The

Markus Venzin, Carsten Rasner, and
Volker Mahnke

The Strategy Process

A Practical Handbook for Implementation
in Business

CYAN|CAMPUS

Copyright © 2005 Campus Verlag GmbH, Frankfurt/Main

First published in German as *Der Strategieprozess: Praxishandbuch zur Umsetzung im Unternehmen by* Campus Verlag, Frankfurt/Main, 2003

This translation first published in Great Britain in 2005 by
Cyan/Campus Books, an imprint of

Cyan Communications Limited
4.3 The Ziggurat
60–66 Saffron Hill
London EC1N 8QX
www.cyanbooks.com

A CIP record for this book is available from the British Library

ISBN 1-904879-11-X

Translated and typeset by Cambridge Publishing Management
(Translators: Rae Walter, Andrew Wilson, and John Kelly)

Printed and bound in Great Britain by
TJ International, Padstow, Cornwall

Contents

A Plea for Expert Management

Sometimes management theory deteriorates into empty words. The thousands of meaningless buzzwords, fashionable tools, and simplifying checklists that supposedly enrich our everyday working lives are of dubious benefit. The models and buzzwords range from the oversimplified to the overtheoretical – from glib charlatanism to unworldly academicism.

The purpose of this book is to provide entrepreneurs and managers with the essential help they need. It combines a systematically constructed toolbox with all the relevant techniques of modern management. By this we mean the tools that have proved their worth over the years, integrated into a strategic process. In order to do this, we have deliberately made reductions. You will not find 333 checklists for practical management to guide you from A (apprentices' mistakes) to z (zero-based budgeting), but you will find the essential basic methods that have maintained their place in both entrepreneurial practice and academic discussion.

We have also cut out fashionable management trends. The customer care and customer relations that the medium-sized company of 20 years ago took for granted should be the same or even better when known as customer relationship management (CRM). This is precisely the area in which we will be differentiating and on which we will be focusing.

What matters is the number of tools to be employed, the degree of detail, and the right time to use them.

- Which tools are relevant? That is, what is both academically sound and viable in practice?
- When does analysis deliver the right results, and what must be watched out for when doing it?

- How does a strategic management process operate, and at what point should functional areas be integrated?

This book will provide you with comprehensive answers and constitutes a guide to the challenges of everyday management. We are convinced that entrepreneurial practice can benefit greatly from academically sound methods, so we have also included the theoretical basis and the categorization and systematization of our recommendations.

What we want to pass on to you is expertise in process management. When you have finished reading, you should be able to manage strategy processes systematically. You should know what strategic alternatives are available to you, which tools you should employ in which phase, and how to deal intelligently and responsibly with the "human factor." The strategy process is the central theme of this book. In practice, it will provide you with a logical structure for developing and implementing strategic initiatives. "What do I do when?" and "What results should I expect to achieve?" are the questions determining each individual stage. This is why at the beginning of each chapter you will find a short introduction summarizing the formulation of the main processes. At the end of each stage, we set out the results you should have achieved.

To a certain extent, this book is also intended to provide an alternative to the "management escapades" of the recent past. As we see it, bankruptcies, stock-exchange scandals, and management errors running into billions of dollars have created a false impression of management. The swiftest possible growth, product designs that are not what the customer wants, and unfounded equity stories generating enormous media coverage have taken the place of sound management practice. People who are permanently occupied in keeping investors happy often have no time to think situations through, try out alternatives to the current trend, or implement strategies in a logical way. It is certainly not an intellectual problem for most managers to manage strategically. It is much more of a mental problem. Strategic management requires patience, realism, and logic. Patience, because strategies take time to develop within the market and particularly within the company itself. Realism, because 100 percent growth per quarter and returns that are permanently above the market average break all the laws of economics. Logic, because strategy processes represent a demanding management task that involves convincing people and carrying through decisions. So do not expect miracles from strategic working, just good results.

No activity is more essential for companies than setting the course for the future. It follows that expertise in the process of strategic company management is one of the core competences of the general manager. We hope you enjoy reading this book and wish you every success in implementing our suggestions.

1. Welcome to the World of the General Manager!

Just imagine you had to take over the running of a department tomorrow, and your first step was to plan to hold a strategy workshop with your top management team. How do you prepare for the workshop? What analyses need to be carried out beforehand? What topics need to be discussed? How do you make sure that the results of the workshop have an influence on the day-to-day running of the business? How do you involve the whole department in the strategy process? This book describes strategy work as a nine-stage process and assigns the most important management tools to the individual stages of the process. However, our main emphasis is not on describing the individual tools, but the way they are integrated into the strategy process.

The strategy process is like a visit to the doctor. There the first stage in the consultation is usually to take blood tests, check blood pressure, and determine other performance indicators. Then, based on the laboratory report, the doctor can start the next phase: identifying problem areas or, if you transfer it to business, strategic themes. If the patient turns out to be overweight, have a high cholesterol level, and suffer from high blood pressure, the doctor will ask himself and the patient, "How can we minimize the likelihood of a heart attack?" This strategic theme then introduces the analysis of the patient's eating habits and lifestyle. In management terms, this would probably be similar to the first analysis of the market and of company resources and capabilities. Based on this second phase of more specific analysis, the doctor will then, together with the patient, make a diagnosis that clearly sets out the causes of the present situation. A prognosis of the future state of health is often made too: "If you continue in this way, you have a maximum of five years left to live." In order to change this situation, a vision of a healthier life is worked out in collaboration with the patient: "Stop smoking; no more liquor or fatty food; blood pressure at 110/90, weight reduction of 14kg, an athletic figure, and enjoyment of life." In order to realize this vision, a strategy must be developed and a path mapped out. The doctor will describe it as treatment: medicine, endurance sport, dieting, no smoking. Putting this proposed treatment into practice demands a great deal of self-discipline. Suggested ways of supporting it might include a stay at a health spa or a period of reduced working hours. Regular checkups with the doctor and possible changes in treatment complete the process.

The example of a visit to the doctor can easily be transferred to business. Companies can permanently and systematically promote their development by following nine carefully thought-out stages, from measurement to implementation. Figure 1.1 shows the strategy process that forms the basis of the management concept behind this book.

In the following pages, for each phase of the strategic process we work out a brief description and a list of questions that can be used as guidelines for strategy discussions. We also assign the most important management tools to the individual phases. The tools listed here include not only classic "recipes" but also useful starting points. The high art of management consists in applying the right tool to fit the situation.

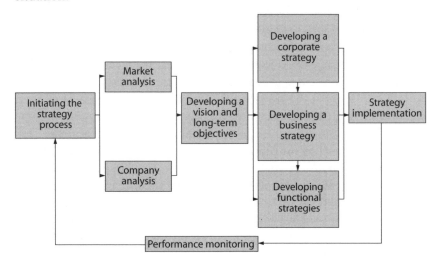

Figure 1.1: The strategy process

Performance monitoring. Experienced managers quickly develop a feel for the "health status" of their department – a feeling that is reinforced by performance indicators. Besides financial ratios, such as ROI (return on investment), ROCE (return on capital employed), or ROA (return on assets), they also look at customer satisfaction, the degree of innovation, and organizational aspects, among other things. In this way the "cockpit," which supports departmental managers in the running of their unit, is developed. Performance monitoring is just as important, as an aid to the implementation of strategic initiatives, as the identification of strategic themes. It is the catalyst that drives forward the strategic process. Basically, the strategy process can be begun at any point: with developing a vision, assessing current strategies, or identifying strategic themes. However, it may be sensible to start off with performance measurement (Table 1.1), if a manager is taking over a new department or if a company has not carried out any formal strategy process for some time.

Initiating the strategy process. Initiating the strategy process (Table 1.2) means recognizing relevant themes, setting priorities, and persuading the company to get to grips with these themes. Business or industry blindness, personal interests, increased market complexity, and operational time pressure make it more difficult to identify and set priorities for strategic themes. Many companies overburden their employees with strategic projects, and do not understand how to evaluate themes

Questions for the management	Management tools
What are the most important indicators that can be used to measure performance in the area of strategy implementation?	Strategic controlling
	Balanced scorecard
Is the strategy being successfully implemented?	Shareholder-value analysis
How can you tell early on if the company has gone off course?	Financial analysis
How do you communicate the value and performance of your company?	Early-warning systems

Table 1.1: Summary of questions and management tools for performance measurement

and relate them to one another. The mission statement offers a good basis for differentiating between what is important and what is unimportant. The mission statement contains a description of the company's purpose and system of values. A good mission statement also clearly describes the markets in which the company intends to be active. In this first phase, besides developing clear strategic themes, the rules of the strategic process will be laid down. The discussions and experiences that take place during the strategy process are usually more important than the actual output – the strategic plan. "Plans are nothing – planning is everything," so the maxim says.

This does not mean that the strategy process has to degenerate into an esoteric exchange of ideas. The development of a strategy can be considered as a learning process, and what counts at the end of this process are the experiences acquired and the discoveries made: strategy as "learning by doing" (Mintzberg 1999). By contrast, a written record of the strategic plan often interferes with the learning process. Other managers and academics describe the development of a strategy as a planning process (Ansoff 1965): not "learning by doing" but "learning before doing." In their view, strategy development is an objective and rational procedure. Arbitrary experiments should be avoided as far as possible. So, not surprisingly, experience gained in practice shows that the optimum strategy process has something of both: "learning before, by, and after doing." Finding the right approach to the process, one that will both present managers with new experi-

Questions for the management	Management tools
Which themes are of long-term importance for your company?	Conversation management
How do you set priorities when working on themes?	Mission statement
How can a strategy workshop be structured?	Eisenhower matrix
How do you manage power in strategic discussions and break through conventional patterns of thought?	Strategic agenda-setting

Table 1.2: Summary of questions and management tools for initiating the strategy process

ences and make specific use of their previous experience, is the main objective in this phase.

The schematic structure of this book and the presentation of the strategic process in nine stages may give the impression that the authors are for the most part following the arguments of Igor Ansoff. This is not true. We are convinced that strategy work is largely a creative act, not a purely analytical procedure. We are conscious that in practice you will rarely find the analytical distinction between the various stages in its pure form. However, the process scheme will help you to understand and manage strategic processes. Just as artists first learn to depict objects in a recognizable way before being allowed to devote themselves to abstract art, managers must learn the tools of strategic management in order to become "strategy virtuosi."

Market analysis. After the strategic themes have been identified and classified, they are worked on. If the market has been analyzed first, the phrase "market-based approach to strategic management" is used. The company tries to gain the best possible understanding of the market in order to define its own position in a way that will maximize profit. So the management is clearly market-oriented, and adapts its own resources and capabilities to suit. This approach works best in relatively stable markets. The first stage of a market analysis (Table 1.3) is therefore the clear segmentation of the markets. If we generalize about markets that differ too widely, we risk only getting superficial or false results, as different strategies are recommended for different market segments.

After the market segmentation, the general market environment is analyzed. This includes describing trends from the political, economic, sociocultural, and technological fields. After that, the structure of the specific segment is examined. Despite its age, the five-forces model (Porter 1980) is probably still the most commonly used tool for this. After the current market situation has been recorded, it is used to think about the future development of the market segment. Methods such as the scenario technique, regression analysis, the game-theory approach, or the working-out of analogies could be used here. Experience shows that, at this point in the strategy process, many companies get lost in a jumble of data and have difficulty structuring the information. Hence our tip: When doing the analysis, just concentrate on one strategic question and only collect data that can help you improve the quality of

Questions for the management	Management tools
Which market segment are you discussing? What are your customers' needs?	Market-based strategy approach
How highly do you rate the volume of demand for orders? What criteria do customers use when choosing your distributors?	Market segmentation
	PEST analysis
Who are your existing (and potential) competitors? What do you know about their probabilities (turnover, costs, investments, number of employees)? How have these grown in the past? How do you assess their strengths, weaknesses, and marketing strategies in comparison to our department?	Stakeholder analysis
	Industry analysis
	Analysis of strategic groups
Which general market factors emanating from the political, economic, sociocultural, and technological fields influence your company?	Analysis of critical success factors
	SWOT analysis
Which trends are these scenarios based on? How can trends be recognized early on?	Scenario technique
How can uncertainty factors be reduced and future developments be assessed?	Trend management
To get right to the point: What are the crucial factors determining success or failure in this market segment?	Game theory
Do you adapt to market trends or do you try actively to set them?	

Table 1.3: Summary of questions and management tools for market analysis

the answer to this question. In addition, you should try to present the market analysis in summary form in a few key statements. It is often presented in the form of key success factors. Take care to see that these success factors are formulated in such a way as not to contain any company-specific features. In other words, key success factors are the same for all competitors. Avoid sentences like "Our strong brand name is a key success factor in our market," as it might well be that the customers do not set much value on brand names but just want to buy the cheapest possible products. Only the comparison of market requirements with the current company characteristics can form the basis for developing the vision and the strategy.

Company analysis. Unlike the market-based approach, the resource-based approach starts from the assumption that the market is too dynamic, in order to make long-term prognoses and define the optimum position on this basis. Before the market-based strategy has been implemented, the market situation has changed so much that the strategies will no longer be effective. Aids to strategic orientation come from the company's own specific resources (Table 1.4) rather than from the market. So advantages in competition do not lie in the firm's ability to exploit changes in the industry structure quickly and flexibly, but in its unique resources and capabilities. The objective now

Questions for the management	Management tools
Do you adapt to market trends or do you try actively to set them?	Resource-based strategy approach
What resources and capabilities generate a continuous competitive advantage?	Analysis of value chain
What resources or capabilities (value-creation processes) are valuable for	Benchmarking
the customer, scarce (competitors do not have these resources or	Core-competence approach
capabilities), difficult to imitate, and difficult to substitute?	Knowledge management
How are your resources exploited by your capabilities to enable you to offer products and services on the market?	
How does the current portfolio of company units look? How much is being invested in which units?	

Table 1.4: Summary of questions and management tools for company analysis

is to exploit these resources and capabilities in such a way that the firm can be actively involved in shaping the market or even to develop a new market.

Developing a vision and long-term objectives. The next stage is to develop a vision and long-term objectives (Table 1.5), which the company must work towards. Even though the area is complex and changes quickly, it is possible and necessary for most companies to develop such objectives. The challenge is to formulate a vision that stimulates performance and is supported by the majority of the workforce. Executives should be in charge of employees who follow them because they have a clear idea of a better future, not because they have a higher position in the hierarchy. So an effective vision should not be too complex but should describe a "better" future in simple terms, so that it can be communicated efficiently.

Unfortunately, the development of "vision statements" is often a compulsory exercise devoid of any real influence on daily management decisions. The vision constitutes the end point – the objective – of the individual strategy projects and, at the same time, the starting point for the definition of medium-term objectives and annual budgets. So a good vision – admittedly over several stages – has a powerful influence on the target-setting discussion for each individual employee. In addition, the vision represents the basis for the selection of strategic alternatives. The selection criteria for the evaluation of a

Questions for the management	Management tools
How will the future of this department look in five years' time? How could you describe this in short key phrases?	Vision statement
	Strategic intent
What are the distinguishing marks of an effective vision?	Leadership models
What milestones are to be passed in the next three years?	Motivation theory
How do you evaluate strategic alternatives?	Strategy evaluation

Table 1.5: Summary of questions and management tools for developing a vision and long-term objectives

strategic option are worked out before strategies are developed. This creates a "fair process," or to put it another way: The decision-makers agree with the selection procedures, even though they may not be happy with the content of the decision.

Developing a corporate strategy. The central question at corporate level (Table 1.6) is: "Which market segments should the company work on long-term, and by what means?" The core tasks of the company head-quarters are allocating resources, making decisions about diversification, monitoring and running the company units, and coordinating the activities of various business units (synergy development). The objective of any company headquarters should be to increase the competitiveness of the units – and this should be recognized by the management of the units. A successful company headquarters has competences and resources available that complement those of the units, and under-stands the business logic of these units. It is only possible to succeed in walking the tightrope between the necessary autonomy of the units and the equally essential coordination and control of the whole, if the role of the company headquarters is clearly defined and its interventions are very selective.

Questions for the management	Management tools
How does the company headquarters generate value for the single company units?	Parenting advantage
What part can and should the company headquarters play?	Growth strategies
What corporate partnerships should be entered into?	Outsourcing
How should resources be allocated to the business units?	Strategic alliances
What new markets should we invest in? Where should we disinvest?	Diversification strategies
How can synergies between the individual company units be achieved?	Internationalization strategies
	Synergy management

Table 1.6: Summary of questions and management tools for developing a corporate strategy

Developing a business strategy. At the business unit level (Table 1.7), the question is how a market segment can be worked on successfully: "How can the business unit stand out in contrast to the competition and provide a unique value-added output (product or service)?" The business unit is directly exposed to the competition. The main objective of a business is to develop competitive advantages that will last as long as possible. The nature of these competitive advantages will be determined both by the capabilities and resources of the company and by customer requirements and market structures. If a lower price influences the customer in your favor, it is called a cost-leadership strategy. If the customer is prepared to pay a price premium, it is known as a differentiation strategy.

The competitive advantages of a cost-leadership strategy arise mainly from the ability to produce large numbers of items. A business unit opts for differentiation if the product on offer is distinguished from the competition by special features such as design, image, quality, or functionality. Once this basic strategy has been determined, unique

Questions for the management	Management tools
Which basic strategy underlies the department: differentiation or cost leadership?	Differentiation strategies
How can the product being offered achieve differentiation advantages? What influence does our product/ service have on the competitiveness of customers?	Cost-leadership strategies
Can a cost advantage be achieved through redimensioning value-creation activities?	Focus strategies
Can concentrating on a niche achieve competitive advantages?	Attack strategies
Does the business strategy meet the requirements of the company management?	Defense strategies

Table 1.7: Summary of questions and management tools for developing a business strategy

selling propositions are developed, explaining the differentiated product's value added. As well as the general decision between cost leadership or differentiation, a company may also decide to define the market more precisely and specialize in particular segments. This strategy is known as a focus strategy or a niche strategy. The trick is to find a homogeneous group of customers that is big enough to have a specific offer produced for it. If successful, it is not necessary, at least to start with, to decide between the basic strategies of cost leadership or differentiation, as there will be no direct competitors – substitute products at most. However, as time goes on, other firms will try to break into these monopolies and produce specific products and services for this subsegment, too. As a result of this confrontation with direct competitors, the company must once again position itself clearly and decide on a new basic strategy.

Developing functional strategies. At the functional level (Table 1.8), the guidelines, whose content matches that of the business strategy, are set for marketing, finance, personnel, buying, production, logistics, sales, information technology, and so on. Functional strategies are mainly targeted at raising the productivity of available resources. The focus is moved from effectiveness (doing the right things) to efficiency (doing things right). Functional strategies are therefore concrete plans for business strategies.

Questions for the management	Management tools
How should the individual function areas be organized? • Marketing • Finance • Personnel • Buying • Production • Logistics • Sales • Information technology	The book goes into further detail about marketing and personnel strategies. The aim of this chapter is not to present the most important management tools, but to show the link with the other stages of the process.

Table 1.8: Summary of questions and management tools for developing functional strategies

Questions for the management	Management tools
What returns, costs, and investments, derived from the vision and the long-term objectives, are planned over the next three years?	Management by objectives Business-process redesign
What changes are planned in organizational areas (structures, systems)?	Analysis of barriers to change, and motives for change
What are the most important activities planned for achieving objectives?	Turnaround management Privatization Analysis of levels of change

Table 1.9: Summary of questions and management tools for strategy implementation

Strategy implementation. If a vision is available and a strategy for achieving objectives has been developed, it is time to move on to active implementation (Table 1.9). Surveys have shown that around 80 percent of strategic initiatives are either not carried through or only a very small part of them is realized. Resistance to change may have many causes: Often the need to act is not seen ("But we have always been successful!"), the vision is not shared by everyone, the strategy is too complex and is not understood, or the change is not supported by modifications to the agreement on objectives, including appropriate incentive systems. Logically, efficient implementation does not begin only after the strategy has been developed, but much earlier, when the strategic themes are defined. Active communication and the involvement of the most important decision-makers are also crucial for a fast turnaround process.

2. Strategic Performance Measurement

What you need to do when measuring strategic performance: This stage is about creating a management cockpit. Define control indicators that you can use to measure the development of your business. This limited number of key figures will cover both internal and external aspects, and is not only financial in nature. In this way it is possible to have regular and logical early warning of deviations, and to monitor the implementation and efficiency of strategic initiatives.

The success of the business is measured by using mostly financial key figures, which are communicated to the owners and interest groups. As the heads of internal accounting, controllers are responsible for the preparation of these financial data. "To control" might otherwise be expressed as "to steer" or "to guide." The simile of the controller as the helmsman or the pilot who helps the captain to bring the ship safely into port is often used to explain the function of internal accounting. Unfortunately, this function is frequently misinterpreted. The controller is appointed purely as a watchdog, who checks reactively whether the set targets have been achieved. However, controllers should not do the checking themselves, but see to it that everyone can do their own checking with regard to achieving the targets set by management.

Controllers should then be able to produce a comparison of what "should be" and what "is," which will enable the management to introduce corrective measures if the targets have not been met. As this "should be" and "is" comparison is usually expressed in figures, it is obvious that at first the head of accounting should take over the function of controlling. But other departments are also involved in the provision, interpretation, and sharing of performance data. So the central-planning, internal-auditing, and possibly management-information-systems departments contribute to the decision-makers having a comprehensive cockpit at their disposal.

Like the instruments in an aircraft cockpit, the company key figures are not just there to establish that the company has crash-landed. As already mentioned, deviations from the planned course must be signaled and discussed at an early stage. Our strategy process therefore begins with the first step of strategic performance measurement – often called performance monitoring (Figure 2.1). The preparation of success figures is often the starting point that sparks off strategic processes. If figures can be used to prove that the company is off course, managers will be more prepared to fundamentally rethink their procedures. Managers would rather believe figures than vague hunches. So when preparing for strategy workshops, it is often a requirement that there should be a brief presentation in figures of the departmental situation. In practice, the trend in performance measurement is towards considering increasingly qualitative indicators that provide early information on changes in the marketplace. Strategic performance measurement is therefore not so much a downstream process as a driving force that strongly influences the generation of strategic initiatives.

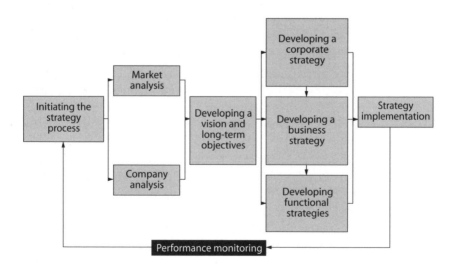

Figure 2.1: Performance monitoring as the first stage of the process

What purposes should strategic performance measurement serve?

Generally speaking, strategic performance measurement has three different purposes: early warning of failure to achieve targets and changes in the marketplace, monitoring the implementation of strategy projects, and monitoring the effectiveness of these projects.

Early warning: Identify control indicators

Strategic early warning (Ansoff 1981; Krystek and Müller-Stewens 1990) has a central role within a company. The purpose of the early warning is to pick up signals from the relevant market area and the company with regard to their effect on the company's target system, and persuade the managers to consider the most important changes. Control indicators will be identified that can predict the likely profitability. These early-warning indicators provide management with an indication of the potential degree of target achievement. This early warning also includes developing effective crisis-management systems and an ex ante readiness to react, which will protect the company from being taken by surprise.

Implementation monitoring: Define and monitor how activities should be carried out

Another purpose of performance measurement is checking how activities are carried out – regardless of their output. It monitors whether things are running according to the prescribed standard routines or whether they are going off course. Salespeople might have the task of spending four days a week with customers and writing a report after each visit. The ISO 9000 standards for quality management are an example of how firms can have their routines monitored and certified. Stricter implementation monitoring is logical, when it is difficult to measure the output of an activity, but the connection between this activity (reports on visits) and its effect on output (volume of sales) is clear.

*Effectiveness monitoring: Compare the actual results achieved
with the targets in the vision, long-term objectives, and budget*

Effectiveness monitoring compares the targets actually achieved with the
management objectives. As with early warning and implementation
monitoring, there are four steps in the monitoring process: (1) identifying
the quantities to be measured, (2) defining and communicating obliga-
tory standards, (3) measuring performance, and (4) applying corrective
measures if the targets are not met. Effectiveness monitoring is introduced especially when the connection between activity and output is not
clear or when the same results are achieved in different ways.

In which areas should performance be measured?

In view of the highly competitive dynamic, companies cannot afford to
consider only purely financial key figures such as ROI or cashflow as
success indicators. These key figures can only give *ex post facto* information on past success, and say little about the present situation or the
outlook for the future. In order to complement the mostly past-
oriented, company-centered quantitative approaches, scorecard
approaches were developed (Kaplan and Norton 1997). These also
take qualitative key figures into account and, as well as an internal
financial perspective, they have a customer perspective, an organizational perspective, and a future-oriented innovation perspective.
Together they produce a rounded picture of the performance skill
of a company or department, like a scorecard in golf. So the scorecard
is a management, communications, and reporting tool that enables
the entire organization, from the top management down to the decentralized units, to be run according to the general strategy.
    A balanced scorecard (Figure 2.2) translates strategies into concrete
actions, and sets focus areas. The chief difficulty in company practice is
not in defining strategic direction, but in implementing it. The
balanced scorecard must therefore be understood as a tool not for
generating strategies but, above all, for implementing them. The
balanced scorecard is most effective when it is seen as the driving force
of an endless strategy process.

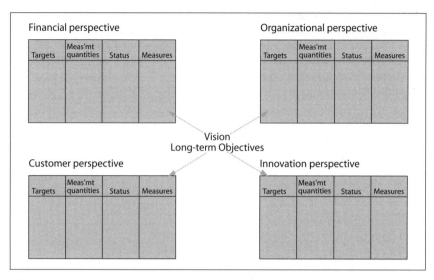

Figure 2.2: Building a balanced scorecard (after Kaplan and Norton 1997)

Key figure systems: Build your management cockpit

Key figure systems (Meyer 1994) have been part of company practice for a long time. Your objective should be to include selective key figures in your cockpit. The danger lies in concentrating only on past monetary figures. The list of key figures in Table 2.1 is therefore not to be seen as an invitation to monitor them all. Different key figures are important, depending on your function and position in the hierarchy. For instance, at top management level, shareholder-value indicators like economic value added (= net profit minus capital costs) or return on capital are crucial for performance measurement. At divisional level, capital turnover or contribution rates are more important. Production capacity or stock turnover would be used one step further down the hierarchy, at the functional level. Skandia AFS, one of the first firms to start working with a balanced scorecard approach, left it up to individual departments to define their key figures. In so doing, they consciously accepted that a comparison between individual business units would become more difficult. On the other hand, different situations require different measurement quantities.

a. Return on investment
    – Return on assets (ROA) = [net income + interest expense
      (1-tax rate) + minority interest in income] / average total assets
    – Return on common equity = (net income – preferred dividend) / average
      common shareholders' equity
    – Dividend payout rate = cash dividends paid / net income

b. Profitability
    – Gross profit margin = (sales – cost of sales) / sales
    – Operating profit margin = operating income / sales
    – Net profit margin = net profit / sales
    – Earnings per share = (net income – preferred dividend) / weighted average of
      shares outstanding

c. Asset utilization and efficiency
    – Total assets turnover = sales / average total assets
    – Cash turnover = sales / average cash and cash equivalents
    – Fixed asset turnover = sales / average current liabilities
    – Working capital turnover = sales / average working capital

d. Liquidity
    – Currrent ratio = current assets / current liabilities
    – Working capital = current assets – current liabilities
    – Acid-test (quick) ratio = (cash + cash equivalents + marketable securities +
      accounts receivable) / current liabilities
    – Inventory turnover = cost of sales / average inventory
    – Operating cycle = days to sell inventory + collection period

e. Capital structure and solvency
    – Total debt ratio = total liabilities / total assets
    – Long-term debt to equity = long-term liabilities / shareholders' equity
    – Financial leverage index = ROCE / ROA

f. Financial market
    – Price-to-earnings = market price per common share / earnings per share
    – Price-to-book = market price per common share / book value per common
      share
    – Earnings yield = earnings per share / market price
    – Dividend yield = annual cash dividends per common share / market price
      per common share

Table 2.1: Selected key figures for the financial performance analysis
(source: Bernstein and Wild, *Financial Statement Analysis: Theory,
Application, and Interpretation*)

Financial perspective: How most owners measure success

Traditional approaches to performance measurement look at figures from the statement of operating results (accounting) and the financial statement (finance). The statement of operating results can be further subdivided into cost accounting (cost-group accounting, cost-center accounting, cost-unit accounting, short-term success accounting, cost-calculation accounting), and the financial statement (keeping accounts, a balance sheet, an income statement). The financial statement is mainly concerned with liquidity calculation (cashflow, investment and disinvestment, financing and definancing). The financial perspective mainly measures the extent to which the company has generated value for the owners. Of course, other interest groups, such as the state or the distributors, also have a strong financial interest in the company's financial performance. Basically, three different objectives can be distinguished within the financial perspective: profitability, liquidity, and the financial stability of the company. Measurements must be determined for each category of objective. For example, financial strength through internally raised capital as a strategic target will be measured by cashflow.

Customer perspective: Direct your measurement quantities towards customer requirements

The customer perspective (Table 2.2) measures the extent to which the company has met or even exceeded customer expectations. Guidelines expressed in general terms like "Our aim is always to fulfill our customers' wishes" must be translated into concrete targets. It seems to be harder to define concrete targets here than in the financial perspective, as qualitative aspects also have to be measured. In the customer perspective, the strategy is translated into targets and measurements relevant to customers and markets. For this reason, a number of target systems must be developed for different customer groups with different expectations. Examples of target figures for the customer perspective are market share, customer loyalty, customer satisfaction, customer profitability, or the rate of customer acquisition. Customer satisfaction can be measured using figures such as the number of customer complaints, the rate of follow-up orders, or the number of reference customers. Customer surveys or mystery shopping can provide a detailed picture of their satisfaction. IBM and other large firms have already been conducting extensive customer-satisfaction surveys for decades, so they can also spot developing trends relating to customer orientation. Another approach to the monitoring of the customer forecast is lost-pitch analysis. Ask your sales force the question: "Why have we lost out to the competition in respect of certain customers?" You will achieve important results in three directions:

- company analysis (Where do our weaknesses lie?)
- competition analysis (What competitive advantages does the competition have?)
- customer analysis (What do our customers want?).

Presenting the figures in diagrammatic form makes it much easier for managers to understand the market success of a product.

Break-even point $\qquad \dfrac{\text{Total fixed costs}}{\text{Cover share per item}}$ (by value)

Break-even point $\qquad \dfrac{\text{Total fixed costs}}{\text{Cover contribution}}$ (by quantity)

Relative market share $\qquad \dfrac{\text{Own market share}}{\text{Market share of biggest competitor}} \times 100 = x\%$

Absolute market share $\qquad \dfrac{\text{Own market share}}{\text{Market volume}} \times 100 = x\%$

Market growth $\qquad \dfrac{\text{Additional market volume}}{\text{Market volume in previous period}} \times 100 = x\%$

Turnover rate of receivables $\qquad \dfrac{\text{Sales proceeds}}{\text{Supply of receivables}}$

Source: www.controllerspielwiese.de

Table 2.2: Selected key figures for the customer performance analysis

Organizational perspective: Design the processes in such a way as best to satisfy customer requirements

Products and services are produced by means of internal processes. That is where the actual value to the customer is created. The value-creation processes should be examined as closely as possible, in order to identify process parameters that have a decisive effect on the manufacture of the products or the provision of services. These are based on customer requirements. Targets, measurements, and measures are formulated according to the financial and customer perspectives, so as to ensure that the business procedures are directed towards the strategic objectives of the customer and financial perspectives.

A typical process parameter for the organizational perspective (Table 2.3) is the flexibility of the organization. But how do you measure the degree of flexibility? And how do you determine the ideal standard of flexibility? The choice of measurements and standards to be achieved varies from business unit to business unit. Of course, it is worth trying to achieve comparability between business units. But this only works if the business units have similar jobs. As previously mentioned, in its specific scorecard approach, the Swedish finance and insurance group Skandia AFS leaves it largely up to individual business units to define their own measurements and standards. Within Skandia, flexibility for one business unit means that every employee can assume full responsibility for vacation cover on behalf of a colleague from the same business unit. In another business unit, flexibility is measured by whether an employee can be set to work anywhere in the business unit. Be brave enough to set out your vision of the ideal business unit in a few targets and measures!

In the 1980s and 1990s, the Six-Sigma method was adopted alongside total quality management (TQM) as being helpful and showing the way. Motorola and General Electric were the first to make use of this process, which strove for total quality both in the industrial production process and in the service sector. This means the failure rate can be used as one of the crucial key figures for the company.

Innovation perspective: Measure whether the company is fit for the future

The three previous perspectives describe the past, or at best the present, efficiency of the company. The fourth perspective (Figure 2.3

Level of employment	$\dfrac{\text{Current employment}}{\text{Budget employment}} \times 100 = x\%$
Employment structure	$\dfrac{\text{For example, proportion of blue-collar workers}}{\text{Total employees}} \times 100 = x\%$
Share of staff costs	$\dfrac{\text{Staff costs}}{\text{Total costs}}$
Staffing structure	$\dfrac{\text{Staff costs for...}}{\text{Total staff costs}} \times 100 = x\%$
Sickness ratio	$\dfrac{\text{Total of sick staff}}{\text{Total employees}} \times 100 = x\%$
Absence structure 1	$\dfrac{\text{Absentees according to causes}}{\text{Total employees}} \times 100 = x\%$
Salary ratio	$\dfrac{\text{Staff costs}}{\text{Turnover}}$
Absence structure 2	$\dfrac{\text{Hours of absence}}{\text{Total working hours}} \times 100 = x\%$
Training costs per employee	$\dfrac{\text{Training costs}}{\text{Total employees}}$
Output per employee	$\dfrac{\text{Sales proceeds}}{\text{Average number employed in the period}}$
Fluctuation figure	$\dfrac{\text{Staff leaving}}{\text{Average number of employees}} \times 100 = x\%$
Absenteeism ratio	$\dfrac{\text{Absenteeism}}{\text{Obligatory working time}} \times 100 = x\%$
Total output per employee	$\dfrac{\text{Total output}}{\text{Average number employed in the period}} \times 100 = x\%$
Average staff costs	$\dfrac{\text{Total staff costs}}{\text{Average number employed in the period}} \times 100 = x\%$

Source: www.controllerspielwiese.de

Table 2.3: Selected key figures for the organizational perspective

on page 34) attempts to find out if the company is fit for the future. When considered from this angle, targets and measures should be developed to quantify the company's innovative power, ability to learn, and potential for growth. These future-oriented factors are highly dependent on the ability of the workforce to learn. So this perspective is also often called the employee perspective. Workforce satisfaction, productivity, and staff retention are the three most important target figures. As with the customer perspective, here too an annual survey of the workforce can provide information about their satisfaction. Staff retention is often measured by the fluctuation rate, and is an indicator of whether the company can retain knowledge and key qualifications over a longer period.

However, at this point it must be observed that the concept of the less fluctuation the better does not generally apply. Big consultancies like McKinsey, BCG, or Bain have a deliberately high fluctuation rate.

Their human resources policy is to evaluate employees every two years and either promote them to a higher level or let them go (up or out). Despite the loss of knowledge, consultancies consider it important to keep on only the best workers, and use the pressure of strong competition to spur them on to achieve exceptional performance. Similarly, Jack Welch of General Electric required his managers to let go of 10 percent of the workforce every year. Behind this policy is the conviction that employee efficiency follows a standard distribution: a few excellent people at the top, followed by a large number of good employees and a few inefficient colleagues.

3M is, with reason, the oft-quoted prime example of innovative power and management ideas that lead to pioneering products. That is why one of 3M's advertising slogans was "Innovations: fuel for the company engine." In the mid-1960s, the then CEO William L. McKnight formulated an innovation target that has been a crucial management figure for the group ever since: 25 percent of sales must be achieved by products that were first marketed within the last five years. Since 1992, the target has actually been 30 percent. For the company, this builds up constant pressure to innovate, which results in clearly comprehensible targets and results.

Return on innovation investment =

$$\frac{\text{Profit generated by new products}}{\substack{\text{Innovation costs (= research, development,} \\ \text{production-cost changes, product-launch costs)}}}$$

Innovation rate 1 =

$$\frac{\substack{\text{Sales of products that have been on the market for no more} \\ \text{than three years}}}{\text{Total sales}}$$

Innovation rate 2 =

$$\frac{\substack{\text{Number of products that have been on the market for no more than} \\ \text{three years}}}{\text{Total of all products}}$$

Innovation success rate = number of products that can be launched on the market and continue in the market for longer than a period of X

Figure 2.3: Selected key figures for the innovation perspective (source: www.controllerspielwiese.de)

What principles must be considered when measuring performance?

As with most management tools, sound common sense should be allowed to prevail. It cannot be a matter of carrying out performance checks using as many of the most complex key figures as possible as often as possible. Show your employees how you define success. Measure it at reasonable intervals using a limited number of key figures, and give yourself enough time to interpret the figures and introduce measures.

Repeat the performance measurement periodically

Many managers are convinced that only what is measured gets done, so establishing and measuring success figures is part of day-to-day management. In the same way that pilots regularly look at their instruments or doctors check patients' body temperature or blood pressure at regular intervals, managers should become accustomed to monitoring company status. To do this, you should consider not only past financial measurements, but also indicators that show early changes in the company or the business environment. Do not be afraid of giving qualitative measurements as much weight as quantitative indicators.

Concentrate on a limited number of figures

All employees should be able to remember the most important measurements of success, as these factors should influence their subsequent actions. If the number of measurements goes into double figures, they become less significant. So try to limit yourself to just a few. Measure the 20 percent of factors that make up 80 percent of performance. Do not be put off by the difficulties of defining and monitoring them. If collaboration between two business units is of crucial importance to the success of the company, you must find a way to measure the quality of this collaboration.

Allow yourself enough time to interpret the figures

It is often surprising how quickly experienced managers can "read" balance sheets, success accounting, and key figure systems. After just a fleeting glance, they often know if the company is on a sound footing and where there are business units that might possibly cause problems. But most managers have little experience of using performance data, and need more time to understand the data's power to inform. Moreover, behind these interpretations there are theories about causal connections between events in the company. Both the explanation and the discussion of these theories within the management team contribute to the quality of the performance diagnosis.

Performance measurement must tie in with long-term targets and implementation projects

In the fall budget rounds, it is clear that targets must be agreed both vertically within the hierarchy and horizontally with other business units. The same principle applies to nonfinancial targets and measurements. In addition, it is crucially important that the targets for the year are seen to be directly linked to the vision and the long-term objectives. If a company intends to be the market leader in Spain and have a 34 percent market share within five years, then about 25 percent should be achieved within three years. The implication for the following year's budget is that an increase from the current 8 percent to 15 percent must be achieved. This logical breakdown of targets by time is often not carried out and, as a consequence, you get so-called hockey-stick forecasts: "Nothing will change until the fourth year, and then everything will be radically different." It is only really possible to assess whether short-term targets can be achieved if they lead to long-term objectives and visions. If a change in market share is not expected until four years' time, the reason "why it will be so" is often lost in the mists of uncertainty. However, if you are forced to bring about a positive change as early as next year, implementation projects will be given completely different priorities.

The contribution made by strategic performance measurement within the framework of the strategic process: When you have carried out the tasks in this phase, you will know precisely where your company stands. You will have eliminated an important stress factor, that is, not having precise information on the company's state of health. You will have created the basis for putting forward the most important strategic themes in the next phase. Moreover, you will be able to evaluate these themes and – if necessary – take immediate action.

3. Initiating the Strategy Process

What you need to do when initiating the strategy process (Figure 3.1): Initiating means selecting the participants in the strategy process and having them mentally attuned, so that they approach the themes to be worked on as a team, systematically, creatively, and yet in a disciplined way, with a common language and a common understanding of the strategy. With this in mind, we will discuss the company's management image, as well as the basic elements of strategic positioning. The strategy process should be run through once without pressure of time, and should generate new strategic options. The challenge lies in freeing oneself from operational pressure and day-to-day activity, and in getting to grips with questions relating to the future. The strategy workshop has a central part to play within the framework of the strategy process. Compared with the countless informal opportunities for inventing strategies, the formal strategy workshop is often characterized by greater complexity, uncertainty, political processes, and personal vanities. It is important to prevent this by professional preparation, moderation, and follow-up evaluation.

Most very busy managers do not exactly jump for joy on receiving an invitation to the annual strategy workshop. They often see these workshops as a waste of time or as a purely formal process, which has little to do with the "real" business. If the workshop is organized by the parent company, they hope they will come through this form of monitoring – which they resent so much – unscathed. To this end, presentations are prepared and rehearsed countless times. In some cases, two different business plans are actually drawn up. One is to pacify the parent company, while the other will really be used for planning.

If staff from middle and lower management are asked about company strategy, vision, or mission, you usually get only vague information: "Strategies are developed 'up there,'" "The company strategy

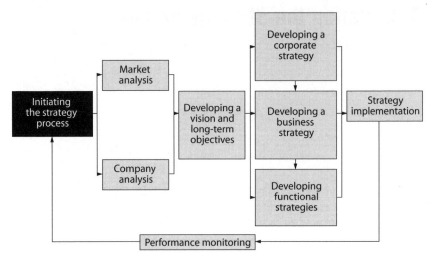

Figure 3.1: Initiating the strategy process as the second stage of the process

has no influence on my area anyway," or "That's only propaganda and doesn't have much to do with day-to-day business." In many companies, it is even necessary to convince top management of the need for strategic thinking. Strategic management can have very negative effects on the motivation of employees and the top management team, if the process degenerates into endless meetings – characterized by power struggles – in which no firm final decisions are made (Charan 2001).

Unfortunately, it is often true to say that the output of a strategy process contributes little to the competitiveness of the company. This is partly due to the fact that the managers' performance is assessed using short- to medium-term results. Successful strategies often do not reveal their value until three or four years later. By then the positions in the company have already been filled by different people, and the results of strategic decisions in the past have become the responsibility of others.

A further reason for unwillingness to invest time in strategic discussions is the unpredictability of the market environment. If a strategic process lasts three to four months, the environment may have changed so much within that period that it requires the plan to be revised. So make sure that the initiation of the strategic process generates sufficient momentum to carry the company through the various phases within a few months.

What must you particularly watch out for during the initiation phase?

As with most operational projects, too little time is often spent on the preparatory and initiatory aspects of this phase of strategic projects. Analyze past strategy processes and try to set up the process so as to give it the greatest prospects of succeeding. What will accelerate strategic thinking in your firm? What methods will be accepted? How will conflicts and political power struggles be dealt with? How much time are the managers willing to sacrifice to strategy work?

Strategy models must be adapted to suit the company

"What happens when academics who think before they act (if they act) meet managers who act before they think (if they ever think)?" Does your management team consist more of adventurous doers or academic analysts? During the initiation of a strategic process, you should assess how strongly developed and formalized strategic thinking is, in order to select the appropriate methods. Each company, even each department, has a different approach to the subject of strategy. In the new media sectors, decisions are made more on the basis of intuition and new ideas are tried out. By contrast in older and more stable sectors, such as the car industry, they have a rather more academic and analytical approach.

The ability to think strategically can to some extent be learned. The logical use of strategic tools also helps untalented managers to develop a long-term way of thinking – just as most of us, with a bit of practice, can learn to play the violin to some extent. However, becoming a strategic management virtuoso and having an infallible gut feeling in all situations when a decision has to be made is only granted to a few managers over a longer time span. And then, just when they have been chosen as manager of the year by the right newspapers, their intuition lets them down, they fall into disfavor, and are fired like soccer coaches (with a nice fat severance award, of course). Only in a very few cases can intuition alone keep a company on the road to long-term success. However, if intuition is disciplined by the use of an analysis model, it gains in quality and becomes communicable.

So the selection of strategic tools is dependent on the situation and the task, and represents one of the most important abilities of a good strategist. Table 3.1 shows which of the many available strategic-planning methods are actually used by the 113 British companies listed on the stock exchange. The study confirms that the most frequently used strategic tools are the most easily structured. So the sensitivity analysis of budgets and the quantitative medium-term planning are the number-one strategic tools, followed by the analysis of critical success factors, financial analysis of competitors, and SWOT analysis.

You do not need either an MBA or a degree in Business Management to master the basic logic of these tools. The simplicity of the tools demonstrates management's need to reduce the complexity of the environment and have simple, clear evidence to present at the end of the strategic process. The study also confirms that the majority of the

	Average*
1. Quantitative sensitivity analysis	3.99
2. Analysis of critical success factors	3.86
3. Financial analysis of competitors	3.70
4. SWOT analysis	3.61
5. Core-competence analysis	2.90
6. Strategic-planning software	2.84
7. Analysis of company culture	2.79
8. Economic-forecast models	2.72
9. Stakeholder analysis	2.45
10. Analysis of the value chain	2.29
11. Portfolio analysis	2.05
12. Scenario technique	2.05
13. Cognitive mapping	1.83
14. Porter's five-forces industrial analysis model	1.69
15. PEST analysis	1.64
16. Experience-curve analysis	1.55
17. Delphi method	1.37
18. PIMS analysis	1.34
19. SSM (soft systems methodology)	1.20
*Scale from 1 = "not used" to 5 = "regularly used"	

Table 3.1: Strategic-planning tools (Glaister and Falshaw 1999)

firms questioned were convinced of the positive effects of strategic management on the firms' profitability.

The simplicity of the strategy model being used also suggests that this alone cannot offer any competitive advantage. However, generally speaking, the ability to set up strategic processes can represent a competitive advantage, but this does not so much lie in the sheer knowledge of strategy models as develop during the selection, combination, and integration of these models and strategic tools within the social structure of the company.

Concepts must be clearly defined

When a management team is thinking about company strategy, it is necessary to talk about the basic concepts in order to assign a common meaning to them. Do the following experiment: Put your firm's annual report under the microscope and identify the most commonly used words, such as "vision," "CRM," "strategic alliance," "niche strategy," or "innovation." Then present the list of these concepts at the next meeting of your management team, and ask each member individually to write down what the concepts mean, so that the team can discuss them.

This experiment never fails to bring surprises. What is the difference between a mission and a vision? If the mission describes the company's area of activity, are we mechanical engineers, plant constructors, or a technology company? What are core competences? How do core competences differ from peripheral competences? What is the basis for our customer orientation? What are strategic customers? The initial strategy meeting often results in a common understanding of the most important strategic concepts, which forms the basis of a successful strategy process. Build up your own glossary of management concepts.

Priorities must be set

What is the actual difference between efficiency and effectiveness? Does strategic management help you to become more efficient or effective? Efficiency means doing things right, whereas effectiveness means doing the right things. Achieving operational efficiency is not the main purpose of a strategy. What use is it to a company if it is very efficient at tackling the wrong projects? The ability to distinguish the important from the unimportant – that is, to be able to set priorities so as to increase effectiveness – is a key feature of the strategy. Efficiency is also required when implementing strategic initiatives. In the initial phase of the strategy process, it is important to create a portfolio of strategic themes in order of priority and then tackle them in a targeted way, thus avoiding overburdening the company with strategy projects.

Operational efficiency alone is therefore not enough to achieve high profitability. The search for product quality, productivity, and speed of production has led to the development of a large number of management tools such as TQM, reengineering, outsourcing, and benchmarking. However, this typical Japanese approach of using benchmarking to copy the activities of competitors and produce them more efficiently can only bring about a moderate increase in profit margins. That is why the core of any strategy is to make harsh decisions, which lead to activities being carried out in a unique way (Porter 1996). The incompatibility of individual activities, that is trade-offs, thus protects the unique strategic position. Doing one thing means not doing something else at the same time. But strategic management does not only mean developing individual activities, but also networking (fitting them together).

The framework conditions must be worked out

Initiating a strategic process also means providing the guidelines within which the analysis, diagnosis, and decision-making will be carried out. As with operational projects, the components of the process will be established: roles and responsibilities, communication rules, timing, involvement, reporting, and investment of resources. In addition, boundaries of content must be set unless radical innovations are consciously being targeted in the strategy process. The company's mission statement usually provides the starting point. This sets out the company's general area of activity and describes the company culture. If the strategy development only involves a single department, some framework conditions may be explicitly laid down by the company headquarters.

The framework conditions should improve the quality of strategic decisions (Eisenhardt 1999): Build up a kind of "collective intuition" through compulsory attendance at formal meetings. Be brave enough to avoid coming to a consensus too hastily through phases of brief but intense conflict, and thus improve strategic ideas. Keep up a dynamic tempo for decisions and avoid overlong analysis phases. Take the heat out of political power struggles by formulating common targets, allocating precise areas of responsibility, and adding a measure of humor.

Make a distinction between strategy and operational management

The definition of the market segment and the company's role in this segment is one of the most important strategic decisions. A rough description of the area of activity is often shown in the company's mission statement. What is the reason for the firm's existence? Xerox, for example, defines itself like this: "The Digital Document Company, Xerox provides solutions to help you manage documents – paper, electronic, online. Whether you run a small business, a global enterprise, or a home office, we offer high-value hardware, software, services, and solutions to help you do more, faster, more easily."

Strategic decisions are based on an analysis of the three most important levels of competition. Resources are included in the process of providing services, so that competitive products and services can be sold on the market. Thus, strategic decisions often cause a wave of less far-reaching decisions. If Xerox decides to start concentrating only on large firms, it has an influence at the functional levels (for example, marketing, sales, logistics, and much more).

So strategic decisions are those characterized by the fact that they usually have a strong influence on the financial, human, and intangible resources of a company. For example, the speed of growth strategies is often dependent on the availability of critical resources.

Strategic decisions also always influence the long-term development of the company, because they cannot easily be reversed. Reaching a decision is not always free of uncertainty, which means that strategic decisions always carry a certain degree of risk. In addition to the current market situation, and the company's own resources and processes for the provision of services, these decisions are also influenced by the expectations of various interest groups. Examples of such interest groups (stakeholders) are the state, trade unions, and investors.

Which of the building blocks of strategic management should you discuss first?

For the sake of clarity of ideas, the first thing to be discussed by the management team should be deciding what the most important building blocks of strategic management are. This discussion, which will take place as part of the initial workshop, creates a common language and the greatest possible unity in the understanding of the strategy.

The development of components of strategic management (Figure 3.2) may help to reduce the complexity and introduce the

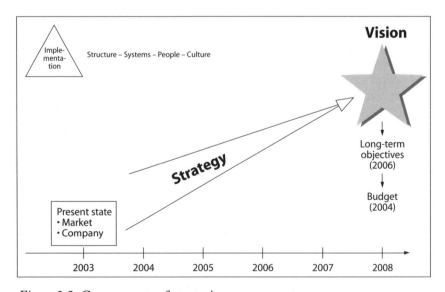

Figure 3.2: Components of strategic management

process model as described in this book. Despite the danger of repeating ourselves, the individual components are described again in brief. So look on this graphic as a prompter that can help you through the most important passages of text and definitions.

Formulating the mission statement: One of the most important tasks for management

The mission statement roughly describes the company's area of activity and its system of values: Why was the company set up? What products and services does the company stand for now? What contribution does the company make to society and people's quality of life? How are workers productively employed and encouraged to develop their skills? What are the rules governing life in the company – what is the code of behavior? What are the company's basic values? A mission statement answers these questions and sets out the company's general position in the business world. It describes the corporate identity and forms the basis for strategic decisions.

Unfortunately, mission statements often exercise greater influence on external PR than on day-to-day actions within the company. However, if the mission statement is worked out in collaboration with employees who do a variety of jobs and come from various levels in the hierarchy, it can have the following positive effects on the company.

1. The general direction of the company is shown in the following areas:
   a. customer groups
   b. products and services
   c. geographical markets
   d. technological directions
   e. attitude to growth, profitability, and social engagement
   f. company ethos (system of values)
   g. core competences and competitive advantages resulting from them
   h. stakeholder interests
   i. attitude to the company's own employees.

2. A mission statement serves as a control mechanism for the company's long-term development. Particularly in the matter of portfolio decisions concerning areas of activity, a glance at the actual justification for the company's existence can stop overenthusiastic attempts to expand.

3. The mission statement supports managers in everyday decision-making, by offering them guidelines, rather like the lane markings on a road.

4. The ideal mission statement motivates employees, by associating their individual identity with the corporate identity. Mission statements should arouse emotion. The Newport News Shipbuilding and Dry Dock Company's mission is described as follows: "We shall build good ships here – at a profit if we can, at a loss if we must – but always good ships." Of course, controllers always clasp their hands behind their heads on hearing these words. But here it is not a case of dedicated business management and maximizing profit, but of winning people over to a common idea, the ideal of a "good ship," for which much effort and an understanding of high-quality work will be needed. It is not just a matter of motivation; a strategy will also be set out, because quality leadership will be clearly established.

Strategic management answers three questions:
What? For whom? How?

A strategic position can be summed up as the answer to three questions (Markides 2000): "What are my target customer groups and what needs do they have?" "Which products and services can be offered to satisfy these needs?" "How can these products be produced?" Strategic thinking means combining innovative answers to these questions in order to find a unique strategic position. This process must be repeated periodically, because successful strategies are usually short-lived. The answers present a business plan in its simplest form.

The result of this business plan may be a marginal improvement to the existing model or a radically new way of serving the market. Companies must be capable of both marginally improving their current position and fundamentally rethinking their position. Finally, a profit-making company should aim to be better than its competitors. A company is better when it generates higher customer use by producing its products more economically or by distinguishing its products or services by marks of quality such as design, image, or customer service.

Situation analysis: SWOT

The current situation is often presented in the form of a SWOT analysis. S stands for strengths, W for weaknesses, O for opportunities, and T for threats. SWOT analysis is not much more than a simple listing of the four categories, which recognizes the interaction of the company's strengths and weaknesses, and the opportunities and threats in the marketplace. Strengths and weaknesses are judged by comparing the company's own resources and capabilities with those of (potential) competitors. The opportunities and threats are obtained from the market analysis.

The most common mistake in the use of this method is confusing SW and OT. When analyzing opportunities and threats in the marketplace, you should not talk about the company, but try to identify the general trends of the specific market segment, independently of your own situation. If you do not succeed in this, misapprehensions are generated: "Because we have a strong brand name (= strength), this is a market opportunity." Yet the company may find itself in a saturated market, with customers no longer persuaded to buy a strong brand name but choosing the product with the lowest price.

Misjudgments like these can be prevented by allocating the strengths and weaknesses analysis and the opportunities and threats analysis to two different management teams. The end result of these analyses may then look like that in Table 3.2. In this matrix, discussion centers particularly on the two fields where a strength matches an opportunity or a weakness matches a threat.

	Opportunities	Threats
Strengths	How can we make use of market opportunities that build on our current status?	How do we make sure that we react in time to threats?
Weaknesses	Is it worth investing in market opportunities that are opening up, despite currently being at a competitive disadvantage?	Which weaknesses must we work on in order to be better prepared for threats?

Table 3.2: SWOT analysis

Vision

The vision is an abstract goal that describes a desirable situation. It is the starting point for processes of change, because it shows up the gaps between the current situation and the future ideal situation. In many companies, the vision is only put together for prestige purposes or because top management has the feeling that there ought to be one. As a management tool, the vision is often of only minor importance – how many employees know what their company's vision is?

Communicating the vision and translating it into long-term objectives at all levels in the company hierarchy guarantees the firm a unified structure. If, for example, "professional project management" is part of the vision, then these relatively abstract, hollow-sounding words must be interpreted for the individual departments and functions. What does "professional" mean for the engineering or research departments? Long-term objectives and medium-term plans will be based on these considerations. After the strategy for achieving targets has been developed, these medium-term plans will form the basis for the year plan (or budgeting).

Strategy: The path to the goal

The simple definition of a strategy is the description of a path leading to the achievement of a long-term goal. In a company with several departments, as shown in Figure 3.3, strategies are developed at three different levels.

1. *Corporate strategy.* The crucial question at corporate level is: "Which market segments should the company work on long-term, and by what means?" The core tasks of the company headquarters are allocating resources, monitoring and running the company units, coordinating activities between units, and communicating with interest groups.

2. *Business strategy.* At the business unit level, the question is how a market segment can be worked on successfully: "How can the department stand out in contrast to the competition and provide a unique value-added output (product or service)?" This means that the department is the company unit working on one or more subsegments that are directly exposed to competition. The main objective of the business strategy must be to develop competitive advantages that can be sustained for the longest possible time.

3. *Functional strategies.* At the functional level, guidelines for marketing, finance, personnel, purchasing, production, logistics, sales, and information technology are laid down in accordance with the business strategy.

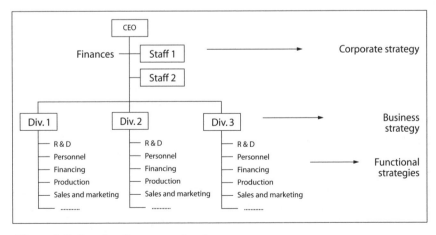

Figure 3.3: Levels of strategy development

Implementation

If a vision is available and a strategy for target achievement is in place, the next stage is active implementation. Surveys have shown that around 80 percent of strategic initiatives are either not carried through or only a very small part of them is realized. This resistance to change may have many causes: Often the need to act is not seen ("But we have always been successful!"), the vision is not shared by everyone, the strategy is too complex and is not understood, or the initiative is not supported by changes to the agreement on objectives, including appropriate incentive systems. Logically, effective implementation does not begin only after the strategy has been developed, but much earlier, when the strategic themes are defined. Active communication and the involvement of the most important decision-makers are also crucial for a fast turnaround process.

How do you organize a strategy workshop?

Imagine you now have to write a letter of invitation to the first strategy workshop. What aspects should you pay attention to when composing this letter?

The participants

The choice of participants for a strategy workshop can be likened to the guest list for a wedding. You do not want to make any political mistakes by not inviting someone, but you want to keep the numbers down to a reasonable level. With the strategy process you also need to bear in mind that, in addition to the political aspects, knowledge also plays an important part. You should consider too whether external partners (customers, for example) should be invited to parts of the workshop. If the number of group members goes into double figures, the organization must allow for the possibility of forming smaller working groups.

Venue

Basically, you should try to hold the workshop off site. The practical advantage of this is that there will be fewer interruptions and distractions. In addition, a change from the usual working environment has a relaxing and inspiring effect on the participants. Of course, a workshop on the theme of "Cost reduction on the operational side of the business" should not be held in a five-star hotel. There are plenty of well-equipped, inexpensive conference hotels. If possible, the participants should spend the night in this hotel. It is well worth investing in this, as it promotes team spirit and makes flexible use of time possible.

Preparatory work

The letter of invitation should explain briefly what themes are to be discussed and how the individual participants should prepare for the workshop. Preliminary work can take the form of key-figure systems or other quantitative analyses. It is also sensible for all participants to discuss the themes listed with their management team, so that they can better represent the department. Unfortunately, it must be noted that in practice annual strategy meetings usually start again from scratch, rather than building on previous years. Preliminary and follow-up meetings to the workshops help to create a certain degree of continuity.

Timing

In many companies, the formal planning process begins in March with the development of the corporate strategy. In this phase, general decisions are taken on which departments should receive future investment and how synergies between departments can be achieved. Around June comes the start of business strategy meetings, which produce the long-term business plans. These are translated into three-year or medium-term plans. Then, towards the end of the year, these medium-term plans form the basis for annual target-setting (budgeting), followed in turn by the individual target agreement talks in

January/February. Of course, this formal process can and must be
complemented by ad hoc processes, if exceptional events require it.

Program

Strategy workshops often last two to three days. For example, they may
begin around four o'clock on Thursday afternoon with a welcoming
coffee. This avoids people who arrive late missing the introduction to
the discussion. To guarantee distance from day-to-day operations, you
can also start the actual work on Friday and spend the rest of the day
walking, bowling, or doing some other activity. If you go directly into
the theme, the first hour can be used to explain the purpose of the
workshop and define the general concepts of the strategy. After that,
the group work on the company vision described in Box 3.1 can
produce a similar effect to an outdoor event.

   This is just an example of the many possible ways of starting off a
workshop. It is important to create a climate of mutual understanding,
confidence, and creativity at the beginning of the process. Experience

- For the group work, five teams are formed. Each team is allotted a different function: Team 1 plays a supplier, team 2 represents the competition, team 3 are journalists, team 4 is your own top management team, and team 5 plays a group of customers.
- The groups are given the task of composing a short article for the house journal. The issue is dated "July 2010." The title of the article is "Wow – I'd never have thought our company could achieve this."
- The groups have until supper, and then the whole night, to compose the article. It is important to note that the groups should write about the future in the present tense. "It is 2010 and the world looks like this."
- The next morning, the individual groups read out their articles, without any direct comment being passed on them. In that way, the team gets a good feel for how the future should look.
- Finally a list of strategic themes is drawn up, based on these short texts. Depending on the choice of themes, you can then proceed further through the strategy process (market analysis, company analysis, and so on).

Box 3.1: Group work for strategy-building

shows that most management teams need at least half a day to become mentally detached from the operational side of the business.

Moderation

The role of moderator should be specifically assigned to one or more people. They have the task of guiding the progress of the workshop. This includes both arranging the general timetable and structuring the leadership of discussions. Moderation should as far as possible not involve the content. However, it is important that moderators should have the respect of the participants – ideally because of their process competence. Moderators may be external advisers, internal members of staff, or alternating members of the top management team itself, as long as they do not abuse the position to influence the content.

Outcomes

To ensure that one strategy workshop builds on another, the most important outcomes are usually kept in written form. If a management team meets regularly at short intervals, the report may be very brief or even omitted, especially if only factual discussions took place and no decisions were arrived at. If time was too short during the workshop to come to a decision and draw up action plans, you should at least set up project groups to continue working on the important themes and report the results to the next meeting. At the end of the workshop, the participants should have the feeling that something concrete has been produced. To round off the workshop, a request for a short statement from participants about the nature and outcome of the exercise can provide important information for the next workshop.

How do you set priorities?

Most strategy tools can be used at different levels: corporate, business
unit, team, or even individual level. This also applies to setting priorities.
Successful managers mostly stand out from the rest by their ability to
distinguish the important from the unimportant – that is, to prioritize.
The same is true of successful companies.

Make a list of themes

The first step when faced with a large number of tasks and projects is
to make a list of themes. The themes should be expressed in the form
of questions, as they represent the starting point for a problem-solving

Urgency	Strategic theme	Influence on company success
∎∎∎	1. How can our customer service be improved?	□□□□□□□
∎	2. How are we dealing with new media like the Internet?	□□□
∎∎∎∎∎∎∎∎∎ ∎∎∎∎∎∎	3. What size should the company headquarters be?	□
∎∎∎∎	4. Is the Japanese market attractive and, if so, how should our strategy for market entry look?	□□□□□□□□ □□□□□□□
∎∎	5. How can we double our rate of growth?	□□□□□□□□ □□□□□□□
∎∎∎∎∎∎∎∎∎ ∎∎∎∎∎∎∎∎	6. How do we react to the merger between our two biggest competitors?	□□□□□□ □□□□□□

Table 3.3: Evaluating strategic themes

process. The following analysis phase is aimed at improving the quality of the answers to the questions. If the list of themes is drawn up in a group, it is recommended that the themes be written up on a flip chart. Then give each of the participants three red and three green stickers (cf. Table 3.3). The red spots should be put on the themes that promise to have the greatest influence on company success, and the green spots mark the urgency of the themes. In order not to be influenced by others, the participants should make a note of their choices on a sheet of paper before they attach the stickers to the flip chart where everyone can see them. One piece of general advice at this point: Although you may have found the description of the procedure with the red and green stickers a bit boring, it is a matter of concern that you plan even these small details very precisely. Imagine if you had 15 themes and had to set priorities in a brainstorming session without any systematic help!

Urgency versus importance

A theme is urgent if it desperately needs to be dealt with. The perception of urgency varies from person to person. In everyday business life, meetings, emails, telephone calls, customer visits, or drawing up reports are often urgent. Carrying out these activities is usually fun – but often unimportant. Ask yourself consciously, what is the worst that can happen to you if you do not do a particular job? How many times have you come out of a meeting with the feeling that you have been wasting your time? Important themes have a big influence on the success of the company. Contributing to the success means increasing the company's long-term profits and getting closer to the basic ideals of the mission statement regarding its purpose and values. Important themes often have long feedback trails, and are connected with processes to do with company policy.

Set up a project portfolio

Using the stickers, the individual themes can now be positioned in the project portfolio (Figure 3.4). Activities in the first quadrant are of low urgency and have little influence on company success. If such themes

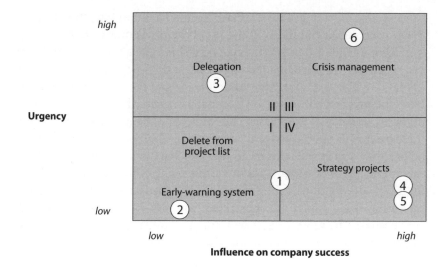

Figure 3.4: Portfolio of strategic themes

come up in a strategy meeting, top management should be brave enough to delete them from the project list. If it cannot be precisely assessed whether the theme may soon become more urgent, you can decide to put it into a kind of early-warning system where periodic checks will be made on changes in its importance.

If the need to act is great – as with our theme 3 (size of the company headquarters) – but the influence on corporate success is small, this project can be delegated to a single person. There is little sense in the whole management team busying itself with this project. In the third quadrant, a theme is listed that requires crisis management – that is, the full attention of top management. Strategy projects appearing in the fourth quadrant can prevent such crisis situations from occurring by having people work on these themes before they become acute. In our example, top management could have got to grips earlier with a merger scenario (theme 6), so they could perhaps have taken preventive measures or at least agreed a contingency plan ("What would I do if…?").

Be careful about changing priorities

Changing priorities means changing your own working plan. This in turn can lead to colleagues or customers feeling the effects on their planning. So if you have good reason to change your priorities, take care that you immediately make the consequences of these changes transparent. Long-term projects in particular are threatened by changes – and this includes strategy projects, as there is no immediate feedback from the changes. It is part of human nature to do the things that have short feedback trails first. So set interim targets that can be achieved, and be clear about the consequences for long-term targets if operational projects are give higher priority.

Create space for strategy projects

Try sometime to keep a written record, every evening for a week, of what you have done during the day. You will see that you have achieved about 80 percent of the effect in about 20 percent of the time. Time has various properties. A period of 15 minutes in the jacuzzi goes faster than one of 15 minutes at the dentist's. In the first hour after lunch you might be more productive than at four o'clock in the afternoon. In an uninterrupted two-hour block of time, you get much more done than in two hours made up of short scraps of time with interruptions in between. You waste your time if you do something wrong or unnecessary. But you also waste time when you do the right thing in the wrong way. Even though it is often said that lack of time is a big problem, in our opinion, lack of time is not a problem but a symptom – a symptom of imprecise goals, wrong priorities, and bad planning.

How can the effect of the strategy process be strengthened?

Strategic management is not an exact science, even though so many (mostly English-speaking) scientific journals try to convince us of the opposite with their focus on quantitative analysis. Strategic management is, to a very great extent, the art of making and implementing the right decisions. This ability cannot be passed on in its entirety by way of theoretical concepts in books. To become a strategic-thinking virtuoso takes more than just learning the technical tools of the trade. Through practical experience or indirectly through discussion of case studies, the ability to think strategically is being slowly and often unconsciously developed in practice and in business schools.

Structure your thoughts using simple strategy tools

If you ask managers why they have come to a particular decision, they will often reply with the sentence: "I just had a gut feeling." This feeling or intuition helps managers to reduce complex reality to a couple of rules for decision-making. Strategic decisions are often not arrived at by purely logical thought processes. A manager's decision-making rules or thinking models are hidden by intuitive decisions. Nevertheless, in many situations, there is a need to make explicit the logic of these implicit decisions.

Only rarely is the top job occupied by a charismatic leader, whom people follow blindly. Investors, employees, and other interest groups demand that strategic decisions be made explicit and communicated to them. This process promotes not just the implementation of a decision but also its quality, as the individual or collective intuition is tested. The lesson to be drawn from this is: Do not try to impress people by using the most complex possible tools, but concentrate on running the process with the simplest tools possible.

When the planning process becomes routine, the planning tools should be changed

Strategic thinking means identifying challenges early on, working out creative solutions, reaching decisions when there is uncertainty, and implementing these decisions. When these activities become routine, the company runs the risk of not fully comprehending important trends and questions. Another negative effect of very formalized planning, in which the same tools are always used, is the predictability of the company's strategic moves. We often see companies producing so-called rolling budgets: Last year's Excel spreadsheet is multiplied by a factor of, say, 1.05. Even if this practice may be sensible in stable sectors, it is not the best basis for getting the firm fit for the future.

Developing a communications strategy right from the start

If the company has reached a certain size, it is no longer possible to involve all the employees directly in the strategy process. The strategy process then often suffers from too strict a separation between its formulation and its implementation. Employees are usually given late and imprecise information about the outcomes of the strategy process. A typical question is often: "Now how do we get the employees to buy in?" "And how do we tell the workforce?"

Successful companies consider at an early stage how they will persuade the workforce to cope with the new strategy. To do this they aim for four targets (Box 3.2).

An important part of communications strategy is to address the various groups in the right way. Which are the main target groups, subsidiary recipients, and opinion-formers? What is their level of knowledge? What is preoccupying them at the moment? How can they be motivated to support the strategy projects? The consultant's virtue (or vice) of illustrating strategic analyses and decisions with PowerPoint presentations often leads to communications being made easier, but losing important contextual material. So 3M asks for business plans to be presented in the form of prose (Shaw, Brown, and

1. Try to build up a common understanding of strategy throughout the whole organization.
2. Make sure you get feedback about the effect of the strategy.
3. Persuade the workforce to support the strategy.
4. Help the workforce to work out performance indicators that can show the degree of implementation.

Box 3.2: Company targets for strategy work relating to the workforce

Bromiley 1998). They maintain that new ideas are mainly communicated by lists of bullet points, resulting in a loss of clarity and power. By contrast, if business plans are presented as brief descriptions, the logic of the arguments and the assumptions they are based on are often better thought through. In addition, such "stories" are easier to remember.

The contribution made by initiating the strategy process within the framework of the strategic process: Now you have a strategic agenda in front of you. Themes that can greatly influence future profitability have been assigned to project groups for further work to be done on them. These teams have acquired a sound basic understanding of the strategic process and its basic elements, and they have been given a general model of company development through the mission statement. All those involved now know what themes are to be discussed according to the strategic agenda, and have been presented with these themes in question form.

4. Market Analysis

What you need to do when conducting market analysis (Figure 4.1): Market analysis generally goes through five stages. First, the market segment to be analyzed is defined, based on the mission statement. Next, general market developments in the political, economic, social, and technological fields affecting the segment are identified. The third step is to describe the industry structure, including competitors, customers, suppliers, and potential substitute or complementary products. Then you attempt to forecast future developments. Even if you have focused strongly on only one strategic theme and a specific market segment, these first four steps will almost certainly have generated a large amount of data. Now the final step is to reduce these data to a few relevant factors to be acted on.

After the strategic themes have been identified and classified, they need to be worked on. Management teams often make the mistake in market analysis of not concentrating on a precise strategic question. We see that market analysis in many companies degenerates into something to be used as an alibi, with the motto "Let's do a quick SWOT analysis," and does not really contribute to problem-solving. But this kind of sweeping gesture usually contributes little to a better understanding of a specific theme, so take the time to ask yourself what market information is needed in order to improve the quality of strategic decisions. Avoid unnecessary analyses. If the results of an analysis is several hundred PowerPoint slides, you have either not formulated a precise strategic question as your starting point, or your objective is really to get a general overview of the market.

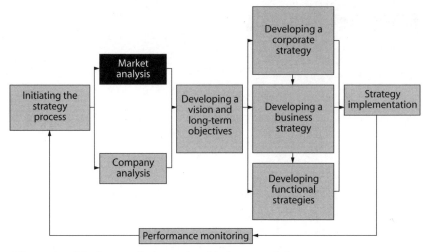

Figure 4.1: Market analysis as the third stage of the process

What are the uses of a careful analysis of the market?

Management teams need to identify the markets relevant to them and understand the market forces affecting them, in order to discover and exploit opportunities for maximizing profit. Continual monitoring of competitors and clear positioning in the market should achieve competitive advantages.

Market analysis helps to identify attractive markets for the company

What criteria can be used to define relevant markets? How can you assess the attractiveness of markets? Should the company be active in a new market? Should the company get out of a market? The test of market attractiveness consists of two steps: market identification and market assessment. Analysis of the attractiveness of a segment is done by answering a few questions: How strong is the buying power in this segment? Which competitors serve the segment? Which future competitors might force their way into our segment? Why should customers buy our products rather than substitute products? How can we ensure that customers in this segment remain loyal to us and do not move away into other segments of the same market?

Understanding of the industry sector and its development is increased

Consciously analyzing the markets reveals rough patterns and current trends in the industry structure. The art lies in reducing the complexity of the competitive environment and distinguishing lasting developments, which are important for the company, from short-term swings. This is often more difficult for someone inside the sector than for outsiders, who watch the industry from some distance and analyze the rules of industry (see "dominant logic" in Prahalad and Bettis 1986). "Dominant logic" describes the patterns of thought or rules of industry, developed through many years' experience, according to which top managers make their decisions. These well-worn thought patterns are often the main reason for wrong decisions on diversification. New areas of business are analyzed on the basis of experience in existing market segments, and this often produces wrong assessments. Even when a company only represents a very small part of an industry, early insights into the way the industry is developing can lead to substantial competitive advantages. So increase awareness within your company that the industry does not represent a given reality, but is something that can be changed.

Opportunities for changing and exploiting market forces are identified

Ideally, a well-conducted analysis of the industry can even lead to the possibility of proactively changing the market structure and its basic laws, so that the profitability of both the market segment and the company can be increased. Try to change the accustomed rules of the industry to your advantage, before your competitors do, or make better use of the existing market structure. Most companies concentrate on

following the industry rules through projects like TQM or cost optimization, instead of changing the rules. There are plenty of positive
examples of firms that have successfully revolutionized an industrial
rule (such as Dell, Charles Schwab, IKEA, Southwestern Airlines, and
others). However, many top managers are afraid of fundamentally
redefining industry structures. They prefer to keep to the status quo,
instead of trying to find new paths to tread, as entrepreneurs should.

How are relevant markets defined?

Market definitions are imaginary lines with which we try to structure
reality and distinguish one market activity from another. A market
exists when an entrepreneur has found a profitable way to satisfy needs
through selling products and services, or any kind of trading activity.
So there is no real objective segmentation of the market. On the
contrary, market segmentation is a creative act and follows different
kinds of logic, depending on the position of interest. Jack Welch, the
former CEO of General Electric, segmented his markets in a different
way from Mario Monti, the former EU commissioner for antitrust
matters. Welch saw markets as a combination of customer groups,
purposes for products, and technologies. For Monti, on the other hand,
questions of price are more important than customer requirements: In
antitrust markets, a profit-oriented company succeeds in raising prices
for certain products long-term above their current and future "natural"
level. So, depending on the strategic question, different ways of
segmenting the market can be carried out and examined, as a different
segment can lead to quite different answers to strategic questions.

*Determine the development of the company by
market identification*

Market identification is one of the most important tasks of the strategic
manager, which has far-reaching consequences that cannot be valued

too highly. The identification of the relevant company market determines company identity. Managers do not talk in vain of "their market," when they talk of "their business." Moreover, the company's market selection influences the capabilities and resources necessary for successful activity in this market. For example, the ability to tailor products to particular market segments and establish brand names is important in markets where there are opportunities for differentiation and price discrimination (for instance, in the car market). In other markets, where products are highly standardized (for instance, in the cement market), capabilities that help companies to reduce their costs through process optimization and cheap purchasing come to the fore.

Furthermore, creative market definitions are also a tool for developing new target markets. The discovery of neglected market segments often leads to the development of products that make a fresh appeal to old customer requirements, and in turn develop them. By considering the questions "What is our relevant market?" or "Which market will become relevant for us?" creatively, companies discover new opportunities for market development. Discuss the following questions with your management team.

- Are there gaps in our product range that lead to our not being able to satisfy substantial customer requirements?
- Is our distribution system widespread enough to guarantee that our products are readily available to customers?
- Is there a new use for our product?
- Can we serve new markets if we have better products?
- Can we find new market/product combinations?

The development of the British potato-chip market shows that creative thinking about relevant markets is worth while. Fifty years ago, potato chips were eaten almost exclusively by beer-drinking men playing darts in pubs. The firm of Smiths, the dominant company in the market at that time, supplied the pubs through an ingenious distribution network with small packets that were just big enough to create a thirst for another beer. In the 1960s, Golden Wonder redefined the market: Potato chips became a product eaten by families in front of the newly launched television sets, and mothers bought them in the supermarket in big packets.

When companies redefine the market, they find new answers to old questions: What customer requirements should our products meet?

What should the product cost? What advertising strategy should we pursue? What distribution channels should be used? So the revolutionizing of the British potato-chip market by Golden Wonder into a market of sociable, television-watching families (instead of beer-drinking men) led to new distribution channels (supermarkets instead of pubs), new packaging (family packs), and new forms of advertising (television instead of direct advertising).

Adapt the structure of your organization to the market segmentation

A further reason why defining markets requires great attention on the part of management has to do with the way the company is organized. Splitting the company into various divisions makes it possible for top management to decentralize authority for decisions. This improves the speed and quality of decisions. It also increases the chances of successfully implementing strategic initiatives. Market segmentation very largely determines whether or not a new department or a new division will be taken into the organization chart. It is only possible to take decentralized decisions if the boundaries of departments match the "natural" boundaries of the market. Only then can realistic departmental targets be formulated in such a way that departmental heads can influence whether or not they are met.

If, for example, the ice-cream market is country-specific (meaning that what happens in the market in one country has no influence over another country), and the company has a single division for chocolate in Europe with no further subdivisions, then it has not decentralized enough. However, if the company has two divisions for chocolate in one country's market, problems of competence may arise and it will be difficult to formulate precise targets for departments. The defining of strategic business units (SBUs) is the company's organizational answer to the market structure. An SBU is a product/market segment with clearly identifiable customers and competitors, who have comparable price, quantity, and quality standards. It is crucially important for an SBU to be able to monitor its own business policy (strategy) independently and to be fully responsible for its own profits and losses. To give an example of SBUs: The Deutsche Bank is made up of three business units: "Corporate and Investment Bank," "Private Clients and Asset Management," and "Corporate Investments." If we consider DaimlerChrysler, it is divided first into cars, trucks, and services, then at the next stage – for vehicles – segmented at the level of individual marques. The Mercedes marque serves different market segments from Jeep or Maybach.

Identify criteria for market segmentation

There are no right and wrong methods of identifying markets. That is why managers use a series of criteria to define the relevant market for their company in a creative way. Market definitions can be based on criteria of demand (for example, clients, marketplaces, customer requirements) and sales criteria (for example, technologies, networks, distribution channels). If managers define company markets too broadly, opportunities for profit in subsegments of the market are not exploited logically and exhaustively. Analysis of the segmentation answers the question of whether market segments are distinguished by region, requirements, demographic criteria, or variations in the product. The purpose of clearly distinguishing between different market segments is to differentiate the company's market behavior in different market segments, thus allowing purchasing power and varying requirements to be effectively exploited.

The first step in segmentation is to draw up criteria for subdividing the total market (Figure 4.2). The car market, for instance, can be segmented according to customer requirements (luxury cars, vans, sports cars, and so on) and also by region (America, Europe, Asia). It is important that the number of segmentation criteria does not become bewildering, so you should combine related criteria. For example, in the restaurant market, price structure, service, and equipment are covered by the types of café, restaurant, and gourmet restaurant.

Identifying markets by means of supply-and-demand criteria often leads to different definitions of the relevant company market. But combining supply-and-demand criteria also helps managers to be creative in discovering their relevant markets and broadly defining them. Market segmentation helps you with further refining your market identification based on regions, requirements, and product variations.

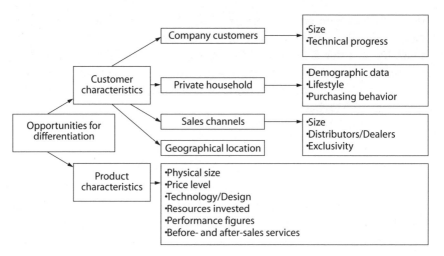

Figure 4.2: Segmentation criteria (after Grant 2002)

Demand criteria are often only the starting point for identifying
company markets, but they presuppose an existing product. By
contrast, supply criteria have the advantage of also helping to identify
relevant competitors who will make it a disputed market. In addition,
demand criteria are often bound up with great uncertainty, if technologies are still under development. Supply criteria attract managers'
attention to the possibilities of basing several products on the same
technology (for example, a bank can sell several products through its
electronic distribution channel) and selling product menus via a distribution channel (for example, telecommunications companies offer
data transfer, telephone, and cellphone services together).

Background studies are another way of approaching the definition
and delimitation of markets. In Europe, they have drawn up the Sinus
milieu model, which distinguishes target groups according to criteria
of social status and basic orientation. Under "basic orientation," values
are described as a curve running from "traditional" to "postmodern."
As there are currently only limited possibilities for classifying people
using sociodemographic data such as age, gender, and place of resi-
dence, their situations and attitudes to life are analyzed in order to
describe fairly homogeneous market segments. The Sinus milieu
model distinguishes ten different backgrounds, ranging from "rooted
in tradition," via "bourgeois," all the way to "experimentalist." The

individual Sinus milieus are described in detail in respect of their customer potential (how big is the milieu's share of the population?), their social status (age, education, profession, income), their worlds of work and leisure, and their consumer behavior. This means that producers of consumer goods in particular can develop the optimum ranges and communications strategies for each milieu.

Construct a segmentation matrix

After you have chosen your segmentation criteria, construct a segmentation matrix, which should relate at least two criteria to one another (Figure 4.3).

The four segments are distinguished by price (cheap, mid-price, or expensive bicycles), the chosen distribution channel (department stores and discount chains; specialist bicycle stores; toy stores), the target customer group (the general public, enthusiasts, children) and the marketing strategy (private label, manufacturer's name). If we examine the success factors in the individual segments, we find that these differ basically in many aspects. If a supplier wishes to maintain market share in the cheap bicycle segment, factors such as efficient global purchasing, manufacturing in low-wage countries, and long-term supply contracts with department-store chains are especially important. That is why manufacturers in Taiwan and China dominate

Figure 4.3: Segmentation criteria (after Grant 2002)

this market. Different factors govern the mid-price bicycle segment. Cost management is, of course, important in this segment as well, but marketing strategies that build up a reputation for good quality are becoming even more important.

Test the segment boundaries

Segment boundaries can be widely or narrowly drawn. This decision will be influenced by the similarity of the success factors. In our example of the American bicycle industry, the success factors in the children's bicycle market are similar to those in the cheap bicycle segment. It is worth striving for if cost advantages can be achieved as a result, because the success factors of the different segments are almost indistinguishable. But too broad a segmentation also entails risks. For example, working jointly on mid-price bicycles and luxury bicycles can reduce costs by scale effects. However, joint marketing can damage the good reputation of a brand name in the luxury segment. That is why, when Mercedes launched the small Smart model, they avoided allowing the name to be clearly linked with the prestige marque in the market. Communication and distribution were strictly separated. Volkswagen chose a different strategy for the prestige model Phaeton. The vehicle was deliberately built as a flagship for a marque that once produced "the people's car." As there is no question of the average consumer having the money for a luxury vehicle, vw will have to convince the top class of consumers that the firm who built the Beetle can also produce prestige cars. At any rate, for the driver of a Golf or a Lupo, the effects of the image are positive. For this consumer group, the Phaeton raises the whole brand reputation.

What influence do general segment factors exercise?

The marketplace and the changes in it influence the company's business activity in respect of profitability and the basis for management decisions. The core problem in this phase of the strategy process lies in reducing the huge external complexity and uncertainty. When analyzing general segment factors, the risk of losing your way and producing nothing but a lot of hot air is particularly great. Consider carefully whether a trend analysis or other market information really can substantially improve the quality of your strategic decisions.

Analyze your interest groups (stakeholders)

Companies often consider the owners to be their only interest group. The possible consequences of this have been shown by events such as the planned sinking of the Brent Spa oil rig by Shell. Overnight, environmental groups like Greenpeace became the most important interest groups. To prevent such surprises (Shell was surprised by the importance of the Greenpeace interest group), all groups that might possibly have an interest in the company should be listed and sorted according to their power to influence, and the nature and strength of their interest. The list in Table 4.1 may help as a starting point.

Stakeholder	Definition	Nature/Strength of interest	Influence on the company	Communications strategy

Table 4.1: Stakeholder classification

This list can then be converted into a stakeholder matrix (see Figure 4.4), enabling stakeholder groups to be classified.

- A stakeholders have both a strong interest and great influence on what happens in the company. It is therefore imperative that they should be involved early on in the decision process and be kept fully informed.
- B1 stakeholders have a strong interest in the company, but no great influence on it. If the stakeholders' attitude to the company strategy is positive and supportive, possible ways of this stakeholder group's acquiring more influence should be sought.
- B2 stakeholders have a weak interest, but exert great influence on the company. The information policy is basically reactive. By providing selective information, the company can try to arouse positive interest and prevent negative interest.
- C stakeholders have a weak interest and little influence on the company. The company is passive towards them in its information policy and does not put together any specific information for them. This group is therefore not actively involved in the information policy, but is monitored with regard to changes in the status of their interest or influence.

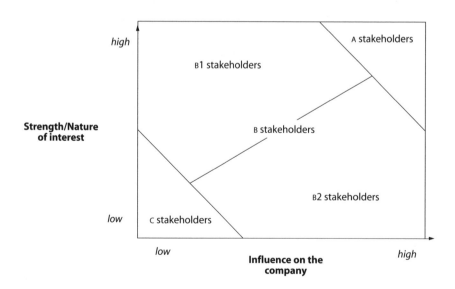

Figure 4.4: Stakeholder matrix

Produce a PEST analysis

An easy way of analyzing the market environment is PEST analysis, which analyzes the changes in the environment in respect of the following factors.

Political factors. For example, foreign trade agreements, employment law, government stability, monopoly law, environmental protection law, or tax laws. The following questions can be asked: Will the tax laws change? How will a trade war between America and the European Union affect the company?

Economic factors. For example, inflation, unemployment rates, disposable incomes, energy supply and costs, economic cycles, GNP trends, interest rates, or money supply. The following questions can be asked: Will the incomes of relevant customer strata increase? How would a possible downswing affect our consumers' buying behavior and our use of capacity?

Social factors. For example, population composition, profit sharing, social mobility, lifestyle, organization of work and leisure, consumer behavior, and standard of education. The following questions can be asked: Will a change in the age pyramid affect our business activities? Will a new social welfare system or trade union strategy confirm the decisions made at our company headquarters, or should we move our activities abroad?

Technological factors. For example, speed of technology transfers, innovation rate, patents, degree of modernization, state contributions to research, or the attitude of companies and states to research. The following questions can be asked: Will the availability of new technologies change our cost structure? When will new technologies be marketable? Will other companies be readier to accept and master new technologies than we are?

After determining the environmental factors from the PEST analysis, they must be given a value that distinguishes the important trends from unimportant developments. Three core questions must be asked and answered by strategic analysts. The more agreement there is about these questions and the sooner the effect of a trend starts to produce results, the more attention the company's strategic management should pay to a development in the environment. For each section of the PEST analysis, you should ask the following.

- Will the trends influence customers' buying behavior and thus affect the demand for our products? If yes, when will the effect be felt?
- Will the trends influence the market behavior of suppliers and thus affect the costs and quality of our production program and our services? If yes, when will the effect be felt?
- Will the trends influence the market behavior of our competitors? Will competitors be advantaged or disadvantaged by current trends? When will a shift in competitive power take effect?

Have an active influence on the environment

When discussing the results of a PEST analysis with managers, complaints are often made about the impossibility of influencing framework conditions. "What can we do about the burden of taxation?" or "We can't change the education system!" or "Now just tell me what I'm supposed to do about these desperate economic developments," say frustrated entrepreneurs, abandoning themselves to their fates. Of course, we do not believe that the individual business person has the power to turn the wheel of world history and influence world economic trends. Nevertheless, intelligent lobbying in conjunction with other companies can achieve strategic effects that can have a lasting influence on the company's success. In America, a daylight-saving coalition (a group of fast-food chains; manufacturers of barbecue equipment, candies, and sports goods; and local stores) succeeded in quite literally putting the clock back. Their combined power convinced the Senate that it would be more sensible for American citizens and the American economy to begin daylight-saving time at the beginning of April, rather than the end. So it got dark later, and customers began their summer pattern of consumption earlier. Early barbecues, the first games of tennis in the evening, and shopping in daylight on the way home from work led to significant rises in profits.

How can the industry structure be described?

A systematic analysis of the industry explains the differences in profitability between the segments that are relevant to the company, by a closer examination of economic forces. Industry analysis is based on the following basic reasons: General environmental factors particularly affect the industry's supply-and-demand structure. The interaction between supply and demand determines the industry's profit potential. No company creates value added without any relationships with suppliers and customers, who all want to share in adding value. Individual firms' shares in the industry's value added are determined by the negotiating power of the participants in the industry. The rivalry between competitors at each stage of value added (suppliers, producers, and customers) determines the negotiating power of the participants in the industry. The industry structure can be described by means of six major factors:

1. rivalry between participants in the industry
2. threats from new firms entering the market
3. threats from substitute products
4. negotiating power of buyers
5. negotiating power of suppliers
6. market power of complementary suppliers.

A thorough understanding of these powers will allow you to assess the profit potential of your market segment. On the basis of this analysis, you can then introduce targeted strategic measures to neutralize these market forces, or try to change them.

Assess the rivalry between companies in the same segment

Rivalry means the competition for market share between participants in the industry. It is generally true to say that the greater the rivalry between participants in the market, the lower the profitability of this industry. The following case illustrates this connection.

The demand for an industrial product consists of ten units required by ten customers. When one supplier meets the entire demand – has a monopoly – they will structure the supply so that the greatest possible share of the value added goes to their company. As a rule, the supplier will cut down the supply in order to achieve bigger profit margins with each individual customer. By contrast, when several suppliers meet the demand, they enter into competition and fight for a share of demand. Now it will not be possible for any of the suppliers to cut down the supply in order to ensure a bigger market share as, if the supplies are cut down, the customers will simply change to the next best supplier, as long as the change does not entail too high costs.

Competition between companies in an industry can take place in various fields, price competition and differentiation being the two most common forms of competition. Price competition lowers the profits a company can achieve by reducing the prices asked without reducing quality. Differentiation competition targets higher esteem from those customers who can put up with higher costs and prices. Generally, you will prefer differentiation to price competition, if customers can be persuaded to pay for this higher esteem with higher prices. The following factors increase rivalry between firms in the market.

Number of companies in the market. The lower the number of suppliers of these products, the easier it is for them to coordinate their activities. For instance, price agreements can be reached and monitored, duplication of expenditure on R&D can be avoided, and market areas can be defined. The greater the number of suppliers, the more difficult it becomes for suppliers to coordinate their activities. For example, it is very tempting for some suppliers to get around price agreements and acquire an increased market share by lowering prices, at the expense of other suppliers.

Concentration of companies in the market. In industries in which it is almost impossible to distinguish suppliers' market shares, the rivalry between the companies is usually fiercer. Two frequently used key figures for industrial concentration are the c4 figure and the Herfindahl index (HI). The c4 figure describes the share of sales of the four biggest companies in a particular segment of industry. In the case of the HI, the way the share of sales is divided between the biggest suppliers is also examined. Imagine that the market share of big suppliers is divided as follows: A (= 50%), B (= 25%), C (= 25%). The HI calculates as follows:

$$\text{HI} = 10,000\star ((0.5)^2 \text{ plus } (0.25)^2 \text{ plus } (0.25)^2) = 3,750$$

If the market share is divided differently, the HI changes, for example, A (= 33.3%), B (= 33.3%), C (= 33.3%):

$$\text{HI} = 10,000\star ((0.33)^2 \text{ plus } (0.33)^2 \text{ plus } (0.33)^2) = 3,267$$

So the HI describes the balance of market shares. Generally, a higher index shows a higher concentration, which indicates lower rivalry, which in turn potentially increases the profitability of the segment.

Differences in companies' cost structures. In markets where the proportion of fixed production costs is high, the likelihood of fierce rivalry is increased. When production capacities are not fully used, companies may, for example, try to get at least a small cover contribution to their fixed costs – even if this means that the selling price has to be reduced below complete cost cover (fixed-cost cover and variable costs). This is in any case only possible in the short term, because in the long term a cover contribution to fixed costs must be included in the variable costs in the market. In industries with a high scale effect (fixed costs per item are reduced on large volumes of sales), companies will fight hard for market share, because it is above all a large market share that makes it possible to reduce costs.

Standardization of products. The more alike the products of the suppliers within an industry are, the greater the likelihood of price competition. So, for example, suppliers of sugar or other standardizable products are often plagued by price wars. If changing from one product to another only entails a small cost, and prices and the components supplied are easily monitored, the rivalry between two companies in the same segment will become fiercer.

Strong barriers to withdrawal from the market. In industries with strong barriers to withdrawal from the market, companies will fight harder against their competitors. If activity in one segment of the market requires investments that have no value outside a specialized industrial use, it will increase the company's motivation to compete fiercely, as this is the only way the investment that has been made can be redeemed. Who would be likely to fight harder for market share in the transit traffic between England and France: Eurotunnel or Euroferry? Taking a company into a situation from which there is no return may in certain circumstances be a method of increasing that company's aggressiveness. Imagine two enemy armies fighting over an island. Each army controls one side of the only two bridges. If one general now decides to storm the island and have the bridge destroyed behind his army, his soldiers will probably be more motivated to fight than those who have left open the strategic option of retreat.

Keep a watch on firms that may be preparing to enter the market

High profitability in markets often results in new competitors entering the market. This has a negative influence on the profitability of current participants in the market in two ways. First, a successful market entry will reduce the market share of the current participants. If there is weak market growth, it will become more and more difficult to achieve cost reductions through scale effects. Second, the increased rivalry in the market puts pressure on the achievable profit margins. The following criteria will explain the probability of a new competitor entering the market.

Government restrictions and legal viewpoints. Many markets are subject to restrictions intended to protect consumers. For example, in most countries, the market entry of a taxi company is linked to obtaining a license, the number of pharmacies and doctors is regulated by the number of inhabitants in the region, and medicines are protected by patents. Regulated markets make it more difficult for new competitors to enter.

Minimum scale efficiency or market size. The total demand for a product only allows a certain number of companies to operate with scale efficiency. This is usually the case when an industry has high fixed costs, such as the aircraft industry (Boeing and Airbus). In such industries, entry into the market is made more difficult by huge fixed costs and investments, which have to be financed by a high number of items.

Customer brand loyalty. If a company succeeds in building up a brand name that its current customer strata can identify with, market entry for new competitors is made harder.

Learning-curve effects indicate cost advantages based on learning processes in production. Observations have shown that learning processes in production with increasing output lead to a substantial reduction in costs. When learning curves result in cost reductions, the market entry of companies that do not have access to these learning curves is made more difficult.

Network externalities. Network externalities come into the picture when the customer's consumption is dependent on other consumers making use of the product at the same time. For example, the use of a word-processing program is determined by the number of other users with whom data can be exchanged in the same format. The more consumers buy the same software package, the greater the usefulness for the individual user. If such positive network externalities exist, market entry is made more difficult for new competitors.

Reputation of market participants with regard to preparedness to take risks. The calculation of the market entry of potential participants is based on the market-entry costs and the expected profit potential. Market-entry costs include such things as investment in market-specific production capacity, acquisition of rights, and marketing campaigns. The higher the proportion of investments lost through unsuccessful market entry, the riskier a planned market entry becomes. Moreover, the current participants will try everything to frighten off potential participants. A particularly effective means of doing this is investing in production capacity (the equivalent of destroying the bridge in the last example) and announcing a price war. The more aggressively the companies in this industry have acted in the past, the smaller the expected profits of the new entrants become and the more credible the scare tactics are.

Assess the effect of substitute products and complementary products on the competition

Substitute products meet a certain customer requirement in a radically different way from conventional products. Which substitute products could put pressure on the ferries of the Scandinavian Stena Line?

Aircraft, tunnels, or bridges also enable customers to cross the sea. If the customer's need is to see another person, even videoconferencing could represent a substitute product. In the extreme case, cheaper alcohol could be regarded as a substitute product. If the state were to substantially reduce the tax on alcohol on the mainland, a few passengers would probably drop out, because for many people cheap alcohol is the only reason for using a ferry. How many people stay on the ferry at the port of arrival in Scandinavia and travel straight back, slightly drunk?

The price customers are prepared to pay for a product depends on the quality and availability of substitute products. If, as with cigarettes for example, no substitute products are available, consumers are not particularly price-sensitive. This means that the price of cigarettes can be raised without the total demand going down. But if substitutes offer the customer the same or similar benefits, as is the case with glasses and contact lenses for instance, customers react to price rises by changing to the substitute product.

The core questions for the market analyst are therefore: Are substitute products available? Will our customers react to price rises by changing to some substitute product? How quickly will this happen? The availability of substitutes thus limits the company's room to maneuver when negotiating the price structure, as a price rise will result in a fall in demand. Unlike substitutes, the availability of complementary products raises the demand for products. For example, the demand for software is increased by the availability of suitable hardware, as consumers need both to structure business processes effectively with information technology. In other words, if customer use is dependent on the availability of a complementary product, the demand for your products will be increased by a complementary supplier. However, if your products are comparable to substitute products, you are threatened with a reduction in demand for your products.

Assess the negotiating power of suppliers and buyers

Because the negotiating power of suppliers and buyers of industrial products is mutually dependent (the greater the negotiating power of the buyer, the smaller is that of the seller), the following description is restricted to the factors determining the negotiating power of buyers, namely price sensitivity and relative negotiating power.

Buyers' price sensitivity. The greater the proportion of an input cost in relation to all other input costs, the greater the price sensitivity of buyers. Drink manufacturers are very price-sensitive with regard to glass bottles and aluminum cans, which constitute a large proportion of the market price of bottled drinks. By contrast, the cost of the contents, water for instance, hardly comes into the picture. The availability of substitutes (for example, sugar and sweeteners) increases the buyers' price sensitivity. The fiercer the competition between buyers, the more pressure there is on purchase prices. The more buyers are dependent on certain inputs that have a big influence on the quality of the end product, the less lower purchase prices at the expense of quality will be taken into account.

Relative negotiating power. The relative concentration on upstream and downstream marketing activities determines the relationships of dependency, and thus the negotiating power in vertical contractual relationships between buyers and sellers. The negotiating power of microchip suppliers is greater, the more computer manufacturers use their microchips. Generally the negotiating power of buyers depends on the question: Can we manage without particular suppliers, still market our products, and so terminate supplier contracts that do not suit us? Attention should be paid to the size and concentration of buyers and sellers. The fewer buyers the suppliers are faced with and the more individual buyers take from the suppliers, the greater the negotiating power of the buyers. The availability of information also plays an important part. The better the buyers understand the suppliers' prices, products, and costs, the greater their negotiating power. In order to increase their negotiating power, buyers can threaten to acquire new suppliers or to begin manufacturing the required products themselves.

Keep an eye on your competitors: "Competitor intelligence"

Analysis of the competition refers to both current and future competitors, and prepares strategic responses to possible challenges. The following key questions guide managers in their analysis: Who are our competitors? What assumptions about the market are the competitors starting from? What are their objectives? How will they pursue their objectives? How do we assess the potential threat? When and how should we react?

Unlike the analysis of rivalry, which concentrates on the structure of the competition, the analysis of the competition helps you to determine individual competitors and assess the potential threat from them. Faced with technological change and dynamic markets, a company must not assume that market boundaries are clearly defined and that competitors will restrict themselves to the acquisition of market share. Competitors from other sectors may enter the market; technological changes frequently cause new substitute products to emerge; competitors try to use their capabilities in new markets; and new firms may be in possession of unexploited market segments, and expand their business activities from there to their company market. Careful analysis of direct and potential competitors is therefore a core task of the strategy. A competition analysis will go through the following steps.

1. *Establishing the general direction of the analysis.* Many companies spare no trouble and expense in collecting information about their competitors, but do not know exactly what to do with these data. In order to avoid this situation, it is important to plan the data collection: What strategic decisions must be taken in future? What information do we need in order to improve the quality of these decisions? If the data are not directly linked to a strategic decision, it is a matter of periodic screening of general information sources (such as a patent databank).

2. *Data collection.* Data collection is preceded by identifying the sources of information: the Internet; newspaper articles; databanks of information providers, industrial organizations, investment banks, customers, or suppliers. Experience suggests that your own sales force is the most important source of information – if you can motivate them to collect market information in a systematic way. It is also very useful to watch competitors' boards of directors, top management, or other key decision-makers at conferences. However, these and other sources must be graded according to their credibility. Then collection methods must be developed that

will allow you to generate the necessary information (for example, by means of questionnaires or interviews). Of course, the concept of "competitor intelligence" comes originally from organizations like the American CIA, and is therefore often equated with spying. Nevertheless, the fact is that most of the interesting data can be obtained in legal and ethically justifiable ways.

3. *Analysis.* The large quantities of data must be sorted and interpreted. The analysis tools described in this chapter can be used for this purpose. Drawing up so-called competitor profiles has proved particularly worth while. These give a portrait of the competitor and look particularly at top management. "CEO profiling" describes and analyzes the careers of the competitor's most important decision-makers. Based on the knowledge of their education, important career and private experiences, and past strategic decisions, you try to predict the reactions of your competitor's top management to your own actions.

4. *Sharing information.* The usual ways of disseminating information within the company can be used: presentations, workshops, the intranet, information brokers (dealing with a special area or competitor), intelligence reports, or sales seminars. It is important to take care not to cause a flood of information. Targeted data should also be relayed to the most important intelligence-gatherers (for example, the sales force). It often happens that after a couple of months they lose the desire to collect data for the "competitive intelligence" of the company headquarters, because they never get any feedback or review.

5. *Using the data.* This is basically concerned with improving the quality of strategic decisions and developing robust strategies. A strategy is robust when it is difficult for a competitor to nullify the intended effect. So predicting the next step the competitor might be able to take is an important outcome of this process. Bigger companies can afford to collect data in so-called corporate war rooms and act out certain market situations. But for smaller companies it can be worth simulating a month-long market strategy based on competitor information. For example, the "Blue" group develops a company strategy, which the "Red" group (the

competitors) combats with a counterstrategy, which in turn provokes a reaction from the "Blues."

Strategic groups (McGee and Thomas 1986) means firms in your own industry that have at least two strategy elements in common (same product range, regional marketing, same customer groups, same technologies, similar prices). Companies in the same strategic group are in stronger competition with one another. This is particularly the case when mobility barriers prevent a simple exchange between strategic groups. Strategic-group analysis can therefore be seen as a tool for identifying competitors. When constructing a strategic-group map, proceed by following the steps in Box 4.1.

1. Identify at least two competitive features that distinguish companies in the industry.
2. Enter the companies in the industry into a matrix, with axes indicating important competitive features.
3. Represent the companies by a circle with a radius showing their market share or profitability.
4. Companies that lie close to one another form a strategic group. The companies in the same strategic group as your firm are your most important competitors.
5. For every firm in a different strategic group, think about whether it could possibly penetrate your strategic group.
6. If gaps appear in a strategic-group map, consider whether you should penetrate this market segment, as little competition is to be expected there.

Box 4.1: Strategic-group analysis

How can the future development of the market be described?

Before a method of analysis can be chosen, management must be convinced that it is sensible to carry out a future analysis, even – or particularly – in times of uncertainty. In very turbulent markets, people like to talk their way out of it by saying that there are no stable trends that can be built on. Other management teams see the glorious past as a guarantee that things will continue like that in the future, and only act when a crisis forces them into it. Another vice is restricting the future analysis to a single area (for example, technological developments) or relying solely on the hunches of an intuitive top manager.

Distinguish between various degrees of uncertainty

Strategic decisions are always bound up with increased uncertainty. In principle, companies could wait until the uncertainty factors have decreased, or as a first move they could try actively to structure the market conditions. There is no generally valid answer to the question of which is the better strategy. But as it is difficult to be both adaptive and revolutionary, the two alternatives present management with a problematic decision. A sign that the company should actively structure the market is the great uncertainty concerning influenceable market factors. Logically, adapting makes more sense if the most important market factors are stable and can only be influenced to a small extent. The decision as to whether the company should adapt to the environment, or actively structure it, therefore depends on the degree of uncertainty.

Uncertainty is usually regarded as a dichotomous quantity: Either something is uncertain or it is certain. However, by distinguishing various degrees of uncertainty, on the one hand strategic tools can be used in different ways, and on the other hand the intensity and timing of active market structuring can be better judged (Courtney 2001; Courtney and Kirkland 1997).

Step 1: Clear future prospects. In markets where the outlook for the future is clear, "adapters" who try to optimize existing business models do better. Only in rare cases do companies (like Federal Express) succeed in restructuring the market using revolutionary strategies (24-hour delivery). Strategic decisions can be prepared using simple strategy tools like the analysis of competition, the analysis of industry structure, or cashflow models.

Step 2: Alternative scenarios. If uncertainty creeps into a market, the result can be that several alternative scenarios are possible. The "revolutionaries" then try to influence the development of the industry in such a way that their desired scenario is realized.

Step 3: Limited uncertainty. This degree of uncertainty is characterized by apparent trends that do not lead to clearly visible scenarios. Instead of different scenarios, bands of possible developments emerge. Influencing these is the aim of the company committed to actively structuring the market. Decision trees or the use of scenario techniques improve the taking of strategic decisions at this level.

Step 4: Complete uncertainty. In practice, situations of complete uncertainty occur very rarely. Usually, certain stable factors provide general guidance on technological or demographic developments. In such circumstances, "revolutionaries" try to put an end to the chaos and establish new market rules by defining technology standards or company mergers. At times of great uncertainty, "adapters" try to continue to exist in the market by means of early warning of changes, experiments, and building flexible organizational structures.

Keep an eye on the evolution of the industry

Industries develop – just like products or companies – over the course of time. This development can be divided into phases, and instructions on how to act can be assigned to each phase.

Creation phase. The market is still small and market penetration incomplete. Companies experiment with various products and are not yet sure what kind of products will catch on. This phase is characterized by great uncertainty, particularly as regards technological factors and not knowing what customers want. Competition in the creation phase is mainly concerned with convincing and acquiring reference customers, and putting (technology) standards in place. Many e-commerce companies are at this stage at the start of the 21st century.

Growth phase. If customers have taken to the new company, market penetration increases, as do sales. Convincing product designs have crystallized out, and sales and marketing are targeting a broader spectrum of buyers. In this phase of industrial development, the competition consists mainly in acquiring market share. High market share is the prerequisite for scale effects in production, which in turn make it possible to reduce costs. During the transition to the saturation phase, established companies increasingly try to set up barriers to market entry, as the opportunities for profit and positive cashflow in the segment increase. The telecommunications industry is currently at this stage – especially the mobile communications segment.

Saturation phase. All the same, it is usually inevitable that additional companies join the segment, and thus lower companies' average profit margins. It becomes increasingly difficult to differentiate between the products and services. Competition is then carried on more on a basis of cost advantages, or firms try to divide the market into subsegments, some of which are better served. Fewer and fewer new customers come in, and substitute buying increases, so lasting customer retention through customer service and loyalty programs becomes more important. The basic strategy of departments that find themselves in saturated markets is "milk" or "cash out." Look at the car market, which is subdivided into a large number of subsegments, in which all kinds of strategy variations are used.

Decline. The market has not been growing for a long time, and companies' struggles to push each other out have led to most companies not having made any more substantial investments. This leads to a process of concentration, in which only a few companies can operate at a profit. They make conscious use of their market strength against suppliers, and optimize mass production. For companies, it is important to develop an orderly withdrawal strategy. Withdrawing from a market can sometimes be difficult because of long service contracts, the emotional bonding of the management team, market-specific production plants, or the inflexibility of social partners. The market for energy produced from coal, for example, is currently at the decline stage.

Set up scenario analyses and contingency plans for increased uncertainty

The scenario method (Schoemaker 1995) is mainly used to analyze the external surroundings and evaluate the effects of industrial trends. Consequently, scenario analysis helps you to think about possible future situations in a structured way. Shell was one of the first companies to use scenario techniques successfully. The oil company did not just draw up considerably better forecasts than the competition in respect of oil prices and overcapacity in the downstream value-added stages, it also succeeded in achieving decentralized learning effects on managers. One important advantage of the scenario technique is that a large amount of data is reduced to a manageable number of pictures of the future. When drawing up scenarios, you concentrate on factors that cannot be 100 percent influenced, such as changes in the law, exchange rates, technological developments, general consumer behavior, or the price levels of input materials. These factors must then be linked together to create consistent and plausible pictures of the future (preferably not more than five). Scenarios are mostly described in a lively, narrative way or are complemented with pictures, which makes them very different from other planning methods such as:

- contingency planning (which is only based on a few variables – "What happens if our patent application is refused?")
- sensitivity analysis (which usually measures the quantitative effect of the changing of one variable on the whole system, on the assumption that all other variables will not be changed from outside)
- computer-based simulation models (which need to be restricted to variables that cannot be built into a formal model).

Scenarios are particularly helpful when the degree of uncertainty is high and the company cannot achieve any sensible results using traditional forecasting methods; a few costly surprises have damaged the company in the past; the strategic process has become too routine and bureaucratic; and top management has widely differing opinions about the future, all of which can be justified.

Everything is as it was: Draw up a trend analysis for stable markets

Trend analysis is often a dangerous instrument. For many companies, it consists of multiplying last year's budget in their Excel file by a growth figure. This multiplier is based on the assumption that last year's success will continue in the future. In order to prepare for possible deviations, the controller carries out a sensitivity analysis with alternative growth scenarios and interference factors. However, the figures are often not discussed or interpreted – this would take up too much valuable management time. The result is that the budget or the quantitative three-year plan is full of illusory wishes and inconsistencies. In order to avoid such a deplorable state of affairs, you should consider the following aspects.

- Develop a system of early indicators that will show you if certain trends are being set or there is a change of direction in existing trends.
- Check trends periodically.
- Also consider trends that are hard to quantify.
- Trends can be presented verbally, in conceptual models, or in mathematical models.
- Make your assumptions, and the validity of the trend model, clear.
- Allow yourself enough time to interpret the figures.
- Discuss various levels of aggregation (for example, Munich, Germany, Central Europe, Europe).

For open questions: Develop game-theory approaches

Game-theory approaches function in open situations, in which the players (market participants) and their possible decisions can be assessed in terms of probabilities. For example, decision trees can be used for assessing market-entry options. If you are considering whether you want to enter an attractive market, you should be able to assess the possible reactions of the current industrial participants and the consequences of your entry. A decision tree is prepared as follows.

1. List your alternative actions.
2. List your opponent's alternative actions. If you are not in a field with only one competitor (like Boeing versus Airbus), you can take a strategic group as your opponent.
3. Combine the alternative actions, assess the probability of entry, and make a financial evaluation of the outcome.

Decision trees help managers to assess the consequences of a planned market entry. All possible decisions are entered and compared with the expected reactions of competitors. In addition, combinations of decisions are evaluated for their financial effects, and the probability of entry is assessed (Table 4.2).

Decisions (1) and (4) are in your hands; decision (2) is at the discretion of the competitor. Proceed as follows.

1. Assess the probability of entry for (2).
2. Calculate the financial consequences of your decision encountering a possible competitor reaction, and weigh the percentage (3) against the probability of your entry.
3. The financial effect of combinations of decisions (5) is calculated as follows: cashflow divided by market entry – market-entry costs = P.

(1) Do you want to enter the market?	(2) How will the competitor react?	(3) How likely is this reaction?	(4) Do you want to remain in the market?	(5) What is the financial outcome?	(6) How has your decision changed?
Yes	Lower prices	70%	No	P1	Back to (1)
			Yes	P2	
	Wait	30%	No	P3	
			Yes	P4	

Table 4.2: Decision grid

4. You remain in the market: $P = (P2) (0.7) + (0.3) (P4)$.
5. You withdraw from the market, when the competitor lowers their prices: $P = (0.7) (P1) + (0.3) (P3)$.

Experts know better: Use the Delphi method

Aiming for the target with precise analyses, extensive knowledge, and creative ideas: The Delphi method helps companies by systematically asking internal and external experts to identify problems, analyze competition situations, and, on this basis, draw up proposals for lasting solutions. Basically, the Delphi method is no more than asking the experts, using a structured questionnaire, maintaining the anonymity of those questioned, and achieving a higher degree of reliability by reporting back the results to the experts. The original purpose of the method was to assess the probability of certain decisions being reached, but the procedure can also be used on more complex questions. The Delphi method is carried out according to the procedure in Box 4.2.

1. The area under examination is defined.
2. A questionnaire is drawn up.
3. The expert group is determined.
4. The questionnaire is answered by experts (if the questions are not easy to answer, interviews can also be carried out).
5. Answers are (statistically) evaluated and collated.
6. The results are fed back to the experts, who have the chance to rethink their ideas in light of others' opinions. Experts whose views are completely different from those of the majority of the group are asked to give reasons for their opinions.
7. Answers from this second round are (statistically) evaluated and collated.
8. If necessary, another round of reporting back to experts can be carried out.
9. At the end of the process, panel discussions with all the experts can provide additional information.

Box 4.2 The Delphi method

Parallels with other areas: Draw inspiration by analogy

Companies may be inspired by analogies with other industries, countries, or areas of life. Imagine you needed to develop an idea of how the kitchen might look in 2005. Trend analysis will not get you very far, as the most important innovation was the microwave oven a couple of decades ago. Of course, technology has continued to develop – for example, the networked house, the ultrasound washing machine, or the talking oven – but so far they have not really caught on with consumers. A useful analogy might be found in the electronic consumer goods industry. Twenty years ago it was still important to show off the biggest possible stereo system, but now it is fashionable to have the system concealed in the room. Music seems to come from nowhere. If you transfer this analogy to the kitchen, you can imagine an "invisible kitchen" scenario. The appliances are hidden in cooking niches, which can be conjured out of the storage space in the walls when required.

How can conclusions be drawn from market analysis?

After some time has been spent analyzing the marketplace, management teams are often faced with a huge mountain of data and ask themselves, "So what?" If this situation occurs, one or two mistakes have been made during and at the beginning of the process. At the start of the data collection and analysis, there should have been one or more strategic questions. The segment (that is, the unit of analysis) must be clearly defined, the decision-makers must be involved in the process of data collection and analysis, and the important results must be presented (possibly visually) in the form of critical success factors.

Only collect data that have a clear bearing on your strategic questions

One of the biggest challenges of the strategic process lies in not losing the thread. Unfortunately, in practice you often see that the strategic questions have no bearing on performance measurement, or that the analysis is only carried out to put people's minds at rest and has little to do with strategy development. If you establish that performance in the area of customer advice is falling sharply (because the customer-satisfaction index is going down), you should put this item on the strategic agenda. This may sound obvious but, unfortunately, perform-ance measurement often has no consequences. If you tackle the theme of customer service, you would probably not need to analyze the nego-tiating power of suppliers or changes in exchange rates in the industry analysis, but rather concentrate on the analysis of customer groups and their requirements in respect of after-sales service, and the analysis of best practice with regard to customer advice. So, before you carry out an analysis, always ask yourself if the data you are searching for will help you to find a better approach to the strategic question and a quali-tatively satisfactory answer.

Define clearly the unit of analysis (or segment) on which the study is based

A second reason for losing the way at the end of the market analysis may be that the market segment is not well enough defined. If the chosen market segment is too broad (for example, customer service worldwide), the analysis may only produce general information. Big customers for feeders in America probably have different require-ments, in respect of customer service, from small clients for manage-ment software in Italy. Of course, there are also scale effects in data collection – or to put it another way: If you are collecting data (for example, through a customer survey), you can extend the data collec-tion to several segments at the same time. But try to assess what segment-specific data each decision-maker needs, and establish how far the data collection should be extended.

Involve the decision-makers in the data collection and analysis as early as possible

One of the strengths of scenario analysis is the high degree of involvement on the part of the decision-makers. The collecting of data and the drawing-up and interpreting of scenarios are an important part of the learning process for managers. Do you still know what a mainframe computer system is? Somewhere in the company is a central computer that stores and processes all the information, and sends it to countless "dumb" terminals. Although in most companies these terminals have been replaced by client-server structures, in extreme cases information processes can function in a similar way: Somewhere central sits an all-powerful board – the only unit capable of thinking – and absorbs information from the (dumb) employees. After the information has been processed (mostly in the stomach), the board sends its words of wisdom to the mere (unthinking) recipient of orders. If we extend these metaphors, the board would have a different role in a client-server structure: that of the server – namely, the servant of the client.

However the environment is so complex that it is probably more difficult than ever for a single person to process all the information. The board can therefore take on the function of an agent who prescribes the frequency range for decisions. It is the employees at various levels in the hierarchy who have the real contact with the market. That is why people often talk of the inverted organization. The organizational pyramid is turned upside down, with the board and the management team supporting the entire organization from below.

Define critical success factors

As a result of the increase in market information, critical success factors can be identified. These answer two fundamental questions: "What does the customer want?" and "How can a company stand out from the competition?" It is important that the analysis of critical success factors should not be a fundamentally new study, but refer back to previously generated data. We often see management teams starting again with brainstorming at the end of the market analysis in order to arrive at a gut feeling for critical success factors. What the team should be doing is looking at the individual stages of the analysis once more from a distance, and briefly summarizing each aspect. Visualizing the whole process – for instance in the form of mind maps – can be useful for this. The mind-mapping method (Buzan 2002) is well suited to the clear presentation of the structure of a complex situation. It should also be noted that critical success factors are not tailored to fit your company, as these factors describe what every company needs in order to be successful in this specific market segment.

The contribution made by market analysis within the framework of the strategic process: You now have a clear overview of the structure and potential of your market segment. You know what success in this segment involves. As well as a realistic evaluation of the company resources and capabilities, this analysis forms the basis for defining a vision and long-term objectives. The company now has two options for action: It can use the resources and capabilities to help it to find the right direction and actively structure the market (resource-based view), or it can orient itself within the market and adapt itself to the demands and the competition (market-based view). Most importantly, make sure there is a clear connection between the three levels of competition: product/market, skills, and resources. Point out how the resources are exploited by skills (or value-creation processes, to put it another way) and show up in products on the market – or vice versa (the market prescribes what products are required, and the company develops the skills and resources to enable it to produce these products).

5. Company Analysis

What you need to do when conducting company analysis (Figure 5.1): First, clarify the availability of various kinds of resources. Distinguish between tangible, virtual, and human resources. This analysis of resources follows the description and evaluation of the value-creation program. By comparing your company with the competition, you will be able to check whether there are sources of lasting competitive advantage at your disposal: that is, resources or capabilities that generate substantial value for the company, are not available to the competition, and are hard to imitate or substitute. Attention will be concentrated on identifying, developing, exploiting, and measuring knowledge.

A company's competitive position can be deduced from the market analysis. Price, design, ability to meet deadlines, quality of customer service, and other features of the end product help to describe the market position. However, this level, which is visible to consumers, is based on two other levels: the capabilities and resources the company has developed in order to be able to offer its products and services. Competitive advantage may come from all three levels. It is often the combination and integration of these three levels that protect the competitive advantage from imitation. Nevertheless, the management team often finds it hard to analyze processes such as those resulting in excellent customer service, and it contents itself with stressing the merits of its customer service compared to that of the competition.

Unlike many resources, the organization's capabilities are the result of a long learning process. So it takes time for production processes to become more efficient, to create a company culture that allows employees to work well together, and for there to be fewer misunderstandings casting a shadow over the interaction between various departments. Competitors who want to develop similar processes can only develop

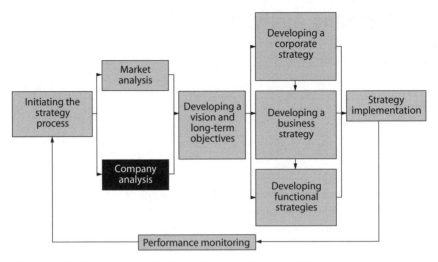

Figure 5.1: Company analysis as the fourth stage of the process

such organizational skills slowly – even if they have plentiful financial resources at their disposal. The reasons for this can be summarized as follows: Efficient processes cannot simply be bought; they must be learned over time. Moreover, process learning is cumulative. This means that knowledge is developed through learning, and that those who know more can also learn better. However, simply pouring more money into learning initiatives is not enough, as spending more on learning does not necessarily lead to a quicker buildup of knowledge in the process.

Why is the resource-based approach attracting more attention?

Resources and capabilities have a big influence on a company's profitability

Imagine you had won $1m in the lottery and invested half of it in the stock market. How do you choose the shares? When choosing shares, you probably decide first on one or more industries – regardless of your willingness to take a risk and your assessment of the future attractiveness of this industry. Once you have decided to buy shares in pharmaceuticals and insurance, you need to decide between companies in this sector. As part of a long-term investment strategy, you now try to assess which firms have long-term competitive advantages and are in a position to convert this permanently into higher profitability.

So a company's profitability can basically be influenced in two ways. On the one hand, it can try to increase industry attractiveness. Industry attractiveness depends on the combination and effect of individual competitive forces: the negotiating power of buyers and suppliers, the rivalry between competitors, the threat of substitute products, and the threat of new entrants from other industries. In the cement market, for example, industry attractiveness is heavily influenced by substitute products like wood, plastic, or steel. Organizational skills, like targeted public relations, the development of new uses for cement, or the ability to scare off market entrants by means of credible threats, help to increase industry attractiveness.

The second factor influencing the profitability of individual firms is their competitive position. The ability to differentiate their product range from others in the market, or offer it at low prices, leads to a strong competitive position. Company resources such as patents, marketing skills, efficient and large-scale production processes, or excellent customer service strengthen your competitive position. All this shows that both competitive position and industry attractiveness are influenced by various resources and capabilities.

In dynamic markets, company development can be planned using an analysis of resources and capabilities

The more uncertain the environment is, the less companies can use traditional questions to determine the direction of their strategic development. Who are our customers, and which products do they require in order to satisfy their needs? Often customers themselves do not know what needs they have until an innovative company awakens this desire – or do you think the electronic consumer goods industry came up with the idea of being able to listen to music anywhere on a Walkman as the result of a customer survey? If companies are working in markets with volatile demand and a quick succession of products, managers can use the following question for strategic orientation: "How can we create new customer value with our capabilities and available resources?" But this presupposes an accurate analysis of resources and capabilities. Even if companies are operating in stable markets, their resources and capabilities can be the starting point for a radical redefining of the existing industry structures. In practice, this kind of resource-based approach to strategic development could go through the following stages.

1. Prepare an inventory of the useful resources and capabilities in the company.
2. Assess the influence of resources and capabilities on competitive advantage.
3. Compare the permanence of competitive advantages with the opportunities to prolong them.
4. Decide on a strategy that makes optimum use of your resources and capabilities.
5. Ask yourself whether resources and capabilities should be protected, developed, or acquired in order to fill the gaps in your strategic resources.

What kinds of resources and capabilities can be distinguished?

Physical resources (not material resources!), employees, and the interaction of their skills determine the value-creation process. Before trying to assess the contribution of individual resources, it would be a good idea to draw up an inventory of available resources and capabilities. Subdividing them as follows has proved helpful.

Physical and virtual resources

Physical resources include among other things the machinery, fleet of vehicles, sites, buildings, access to good suppliers, and the location of the company (for example, a hotel in a central location with a connection to the airport). This category of resources includes everything tangible within the company. Despite the high degree of automation and the availability of new information technologies, people are still a crucially important resource. That is why companies must be sure to hold on to their workers and acquire new qualified staff. The following holds good:

Employee effectiveness = Skills × Motivation

Companies with skilled and motivated workers find it easier to attract new employees on the market. Unlike physical resources, nonmaterial resources are intangible. They include, for example, the company's reputation, customer loyalty to the products offered, and the business climate within the company.

Functional and integrative capabilities

Looked at on their own, individual resources often have no great value. Value added is only created by the company's ability to convert resources and use them in processes. Just consider who in BMW knows how a car is produced. Probably no one single worker. But new cars are built all the same, because the interaction of workers and their knowledge in the company process is organized in such a way that everyone can contribute their knowledge, but nobody needs to know everything. Functional process capabilities refer, for example, to R&D, production processes, customer service, marketing, human resource management, financial management, company logistics, and similar processes. Because these functional processes are usually organized on the principle of division of labor, a company must also have integrative skills available, which can bring the parts of the functional process together as a whole. For example, the development of a new car must dovetail the processes of R&D, production, and sales in order for a new model to move successfully out of the depot.

How can the strategic value of resources and capabilities be established?

It is of little use being able to do or own something, unless you can really use it for concrete purposes in the value-creation process. Individual resources and capabilities must therefore be evaluated in respect of their potential. Which resources and capabilities within your company generate high value for customers (internal or external), are rare (your competitors do not have the same resources and capabilities available), are hard to imitate (how long will it take, for example, before a competitor copies a specific production capability?), and cannot be substituted (for example, another technology that can do something similar)?

Answering these questions is often a painful process, as most companies are forced to realize that they have no resources and capabilities that meet all the criteria. In most strategy workshops, at best the company culture, employee knowledge, or the brand name are put forward as sources of permanent competitive advantage that might be thought to fulfill the four conditions. Note that they rarely speak of employee knowledge or the company culture, but go into real detail. What makes your company culture better than that of your competitors? What knowledge do your workers have that your competitors do not have at their disposal? How long will it be before your competitors have acquired this knowledge? What would happen if your entire development team was lured away? The following criteria will help you to put your resources and capabilities under the microscope.

Assess the strategic relevance of resources and capabilities

A resource or capability is of strategic value if it supports the company strategy in a unique way. For example, an excellent logistics process can help a company to lower costs and operate a price-leadership strategy in the market. Strategically relevant resources help companies to be aware of opportunities in the external environment, and to ward off threats. On the other hand, available resources and capabilities can inhibit the development of the company (Leonard-Barton 1992; 1995). Changes in customer tastes, the industry structure, or technologies can also devalue current resources. For example, the development of personal computers and word-processing software reduced the relevance of the skill of manufacturing typewriters. In such cases, it is often difficult for the firm to build up new capabilities.

Assess how rare your resources and capabilities are

If all competitors have the same resources and capabilities, no competitor can achieve competitive advantage by using them. On the other hand, the chances of achieving competitive advantage are greater if you have a rare resource or capability, because they make your company product unique in the market. So, for example, certain medicines can only be produced and sold if the company owns the appropriate patent. This also makes the use of benchmark studies relevant. It is known that many firms try to use a careful study of a competitor, in order to discover their recipe for success and copy it. At most that puts them on a par with the competition: The companies are evenly matched. Competitive advantages are then generated only if a company – perhaps inspired by a detailed comparison with the competition – goes its own way and develops its own unique combination of resources and capabilities.

Assess how easily your resources and capabilities can be imitated and substituted

If resources are available to all competitors and can be used by them, the competitive advantage of your company is destroyed. The more difficult it is to imitate a resource or capability, the higher its value for the company, if it can be used by your company alone (Dierickx and Cool 1989). So pay attention to factors that make it less easy and more expensive for your competitors to imitate your resources. The greater the social complexity of the capabilities, the more individual resources are combined with one another, and the greater the uncertainty about the causal connections leading to the profitability of resources, the more difficult it becomes for other companies to imitate your resources.

Moreover, resources are proportionately more valuable, the more difficult they are to substitute. For example, the rights to Mickey Mouse
cannot be substituted by other resources.

Assess how easily resources and capabilities can be deployed

Resources and capabilities can be deployed in a general or specific way,
according to whether the same resource has one or more uses. The
more possibilities there are of using resources in different ways, the
more valuable these resources are to the company. At the same time, it
is true to say that the more general ways there are of using resources,
the easier it is for other companies to use those resources too. As a rule,
a major effort is needed to keep resources within the company or
protect them from imitation. A simple example of this is production
plants that can be set up anywhere. But even the brand name can be
consciously used and exploited in various places. So the brand name is
an important factor not just in sales-and-marketing activities, but also
in procurement or recruiting.

Take care that value creation is not absorbed by resources

Even when the resources used are sufficient, strategically relevant, and
cannot be substituted or imitated, the company must ensure that the
value created by investing resources benefits the company and no one
else. For example, a large part of the value created in movie production
is absorbed by the stars. The negotiating power of Tom Cruise or Mel
Gibson is so great that they can absorb a large part of the profits as
(co)producers. By contrast, cartoon studios have far fewer problems
negotiating with Mickey Mouse or Roger Rabbit.

Consider the effects of capabilities in combination

Even if none of your available resources and capabilities promise
permanent competitive advantage when considered in isolation, this

can often be achieved by combining resources and capabilities. If you assume there is a 90 percent probability that your competitors could imitate or substitute each of your capabilities within six months, a combination of capabilities would give you unique competitive advantages $(0.9 \times 0.81; 0.9 \times 0.9 \times 0.9 \times 0.9 \times 0.9 \times 0.9 \times 0.9 \times 0.9 = 0.43)$, because the probability of imitating or substituting a large number of elements in combination decreases rapidly. If, for example, you combine eight instead of two capabilities in your production process, the probability of imitation goes down from 81 percent to 43 percent. For Dell, the combination of superior direct marketing, individualized mass production, and logistical competence in connection with their power over suppliers in the market is a significant competitive advantage, which is very difficult for competitors to imitate.

Take decisions about outsourcing using an analysis of the value chain

Finally, it is a matter of using resources and capabilities in the value chain in a way that generates unique value added for customers (see Figure 5.2 overleaf). The chain represents the company's value-creation process and separates primary functions, that is, core functions (purchasing, production, logistics, marketing, and sales) from supporting functions (personnel management, finances, administration).

Answer the following questions for each individual function in the company (Quinn 1995).

- Do our resources and capabilities contribute to supporting the core and supporting functions? If the answer is no, then these resources and capabilities create no value in the way they are currently being used. So consider if and how available resources and capabilities can be used to create value, or sell off resources that are not being used. If your resources and capabilities contribute to creating value, go on to the next question.
- Can other companies carry out the same functions either more cheaply for the same quality or better for the same costs? If the answer is no, then your resources and capabilities are creating competitive advantage in the way they are currently being used. These resources

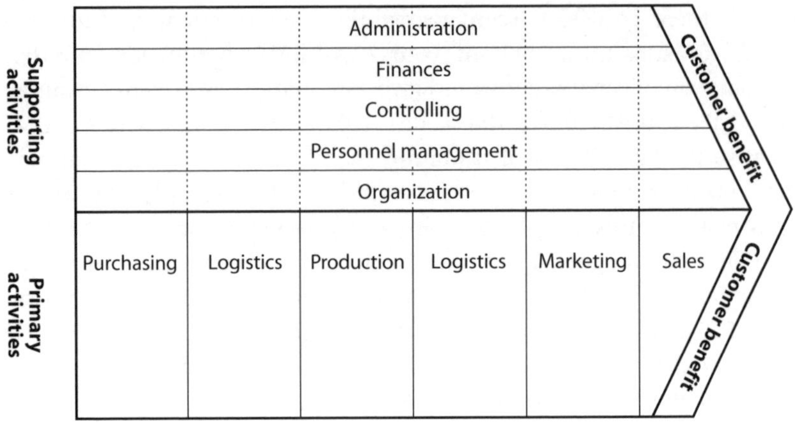

Figure 5.2: Value chain (after Porter 1980)

and capabilities absolutely must be protected against competitors, and be further developed. If the answer to this question is yes, consider whether outsourcing partners could take over these functions for you. If no reliable partners can be found, you have no other option other than to develop the appropriate resources and capabilities in order to create lasting customer value.

A company should concentrate in the long term on those functions that can make use of available resources and capabilities to create lasting customer benefit, and which the company can carry out better or more cheaply than others. All other functions should be taken over by suppliers, as long as they work as reliable partners and do not use the relationship of dependency to blackmail you.

How can knowledge be systematically analyzed?

The ability to identify and develop knowledge, and convert it into competences and innovations, will have a strong influence on the company's competitive position in the next few decades of the information age. Although many companies already recognize knowledge as their most important resource, efficient concepts and methods for managing it are often lacking. In fact, knowledge has all the characteristics needed for a source of permanent competitive advantage. It is valuable, rare, hard to imitate, and hard to substitute. But things are actually rather different in practice, because knowledge does not match the four criteria very exactly. By definition, knowledge is rare or even unique (if only in subtle details). Especially in the case of knowledge that is not in codifiable form, otherwise known as implicit knowledge, imitation and transfer are difficult. However, managers estimate that less than 30 percent of a firm's knowledge ever gets used. Although this is, of course, hard to assess, this information shows us that, though knowledge potentially generates value, only a small part of it is actually used in practice. Imagine if production plants were only used at 30 percent capacity.

The question of whether knowledge can be substituted cannot be fully answered either. So basically, you should be careful if anyone suggests knowledge in general as the most important source of competitive advantage, because a lot of money is often invested in developing knowledge that is not subsequently used or is easy to copy. However, logical and systematic management of knowledge can really transform knowledge into a source of long-lasting competitive advantage. When it comes down to it, knowledge management consists of four main activities: the identification, development, exploitation, and measurement of knowledge (Venzin 1998).

Recognize the influence of knowledge on your competitiveness

The aim of any company is to offer products and services that generate the greatest possible value for the customer. In doing this, the company is in competition with many other businesses that generate similar value, and possibly at lower prices. But how do these differences come about? The acquisition of or access to physical resources such as capital, machinery, buildings, production plants, or raw materials cannot explain these differences in the long term. Even a unique combination of these resources cannot protect a firm against being overtaken by the competition. So entrepreneurs must ask themselves the question of which resources are either impossible or hard to imitate or transfer (Grant 1991).

Examples of such resources are brand names, patents, customer data-bases, social networks, customer loyalty, experience in production, the organization's culture, or the employees' knowledge. These resources are not tangible, and therefore cannot be handled. Their quality depends on how they were created, and is built up over a long period. They also flow into several products at the same time, affect whole areas of the business, and are unique among competitors. What they have in common is that they are based on explicit or implicit knowledge: knowledge about organizational procedures, new technologies, other workers, completed projects, customer requirements, different cultures, events in the industry, customer products, or rules of conduct within other companies. The challenge for management consists in identifying and developing valuable knowledge inside and outside the company, and linking it together in the form of products or services, so that it generates the kind of value with customers that makes a difference.

Identify the available knowledge

Most knowledge management projects begin by identifying and codifying various kinds of knowledge, which then spend years crammed into databases, maturing. If you are charged with such a project, you would be well advised to make your first step identifying areas of knowledge that have a lot of influence on company success. What knowledge can have a positive long-term influence on the position with regard to cost or differentiation? What knowledge can make the sector more attractive?

Often great potential remains unused in the company because no one really knows that it is available. Experience gained from projects or daily work is not transferred to new areas of activity. A certain degree of transparency in the knowledge base lays the foundations for combining, developing, and converting knowledge in new ways. The practical way to do this is by means of electronic databanks of knowledge, but be careful. Concentrating only on information technology has caused more than one knowledge-management project to founder before now. Information technology can and must be no more than a means of support for the streams of information about people. Internal company databases store employees in the organization not by name but by the kind of knowledge they have. Other companies produce lists of subject areas for which discussion groups have already been formed. Yet others concentrate on identifying external knowledge by trying to display and analyze their business connections in networks.

There are even companies that try to establish connections by preparing (electronic) "knowledge telephone directories" or putting "knowledge brokers" in their organization charts. The telecommunications company Cable & Wireless set up an independent business unit within the company to deal with recruitment, transfers and promotions, and career planning. Databases providing information about employees' skills, and where they want to work, form the basis of a global exchange of knowledge. Increased transparency in the organization's knowledge base means that opportunities in the industry can by spotted more quickly and integrated into the company's business activities.

Promote the development of new knowledge

Imagine that in five years' time you are invited to present a report to your sector association. What subject would you speak on? Where would your expert knowledge take you? A vision of knowledge is often the starting point for the development of knowledge. As well as knowledge being developed at the individual level, formal and informal meetings are a particularly good way of developing and transferring existing knowledge. The variety of language in a specific area can be an indicator of the importance and extent of knowledge. For example, the Eskimo language has around 40 words for snow. For Eskimos, snow is an important part of their life, and it is often crucial for survival to know what kind of snow is in question. Try it out on your management team. How long can you talk about internationalization strategies in the group without repeating yourselves or deviating from the subject?

As illustrated by the example of the Eskimos, knowledge is bound up with language. New words and new meanings extend the knowledge base. The American firm Sencorp puts a great deal of emphasis on developing individual knowledge. Every one of Sencorp's employees is allowed to take up to 20 percent of their working hours off from operational activity and increase their knowledge in interesting areas (Von Krogh and Roos 1995). The choice of subjects is not prescribed, but an application for a project must have the blessing of top management.

Put your hand on your heart. How happy are you with the meetings in your company? Meetings are often called at the last minute, the participants are unprepared and arrive late, no proper moderator is available, no agenda for structuring discussions is in place, the meeting overruns, and very little results from it. Our tip: Separate operational sessions (in which you use the available knowledge on specific tasks) from strategic sessions (in which you develop fundamentally new knowledge). The two kinds of meeting are for different purposes. It may, for example, be sensible in operational meetings to come to a few very quick decisions under pressure of time from on high. An Italian motorcycle manufacturer even went so far as to have the finance office calculate the cost of every meeting before it was called. After the meeting, there was a recalculation based on the participants' effective use of time.

By contrast, strategic discussions at Sencorp are characterized by mutual trust and respect. Hierarchical differences become meaningless in these conversations. All contributions to strategic discussions are judged to be equally valuable. The discussions have no fixed agenda, and managers are not obliged to take part in them. No quick decisions are sought. Developing knowledge within a team requires mutual understanding, which can be achieved by developing a common language and meeting regularly. Thorough preparation and discussion of decisions speed up implementation.

Target the use of available knowledge

Competence is created when tasks or company problems are matched by the available knowledge. The competence of VEBA in the energy-supply sector consists, among other things, of process knowledge in the management of large networks and the job of energy transfer. By listing and linking the organization of tasks and knowledge, sound decisions can be made about the competence configuration. How might new competences be created by managing the organization of tasks, for instance, by changing from simple to complex tasks? What knowledge can be applied to new tasks? How, for instance, can VEBA's process knowledge in the management of large networks, applied to the new task (transferring data instead of energy), create a new competence in the field of telecommunications systems? For which tasks is there little knowledge available? How can competences be transferred? Texas Instruments answered the last question by introducing a kind of "library" of best practice, which enabled them to institutionalize the storage and transfer of competences. Competences in different areas were documented, stored, and made accessible to everyone.

Extending the competence configuration allows the creation of competences to include feedback on the development of knowledge. Existing and new tasks require new knowledge. If competence is built up by this iterative process, it will be used in the next innovation-management activity.

Measure the quality and quantity of knowledge, and the knowledge development process

Discussions are the central part of knowledge development, but they alone are not enough. The development of individual knowledge and communication with others must also be transformed into encoded knowledge. The Swedish finance and insurance company Skandia AFS recognized the need for this. At Skandia, the value of these assets was assessed and included in the annual report. Originally, the most important purpose of this was to communicate the growth in intellectual capital to the shareholders. In the meantime, however, the measurement and evaluation of intellectual capital has raised awareness of the importance of knowledge in the organization.

Under the heading of intellectual capital, Skandia includes such things as knowledge, technologies, customer relations, intercultural skills, and related experiences. Intellectual capital is embedded in human capital and structural capital. Human capital embodies individual knowledge or skills. Structural capital consists of the intellectual capital that remains when the workers have gone home. Encoded knowledge is the basis of structural capital.

Consistent efforts to build up and transfer encoded knowledge, and use it in a wide variety of areas, make this category of knowledge an important component of knowledge management at Skandia. For example, the use of encoded knowledge has reduced the cost of building a new branch in another country by up to 50 percent, although the same team was not involved in the building.

The contribution made by company analysis within the framework of the strategic process: You now know whether your company has sources of permanent competitive advantage at its disposal. You have an overview of the available resources and capabilities, and know how they interact at product/market level.

6. Developing a Vision and Long-Term Objectives

What you need to do when developing a vision and long-term objectives (Figure 6.1): Developing a vision means creating a picture of the future that is better than the status quo. The vision is a superior tool for coordination and constitutes the starting point for setting medium-term targets and annual budgets. Your task is to ensure the uniformity of the targets. A vision with a horizon of five to ten years must be broken down into a three-year medium-term plan, and then into annual targets across all levels of the hierarchy and functional barriers. A vision should also motivate employees actively to structure the future. Communicating and experiencing the vision is a precondition. Another important task in this phase is to draw up criteria, based on the vision, for choosing strategic alternatives. If these are made clear before strategies are worked out, it creates process fairness, and the people involved will be more ready to accept strategies that affect them more negatively.

You have probably often heard before that the company must change: "Every individual contributes to change. Change begins with you. So let's get on with it…" Unfortunately, top management does not always make the direction of change clear. Then the word "empowerment" is used as an excuse for missing visions. "We don't have a clue what to do either, but you're doing it anyway." Even though former German Chancellor Helmut Schmidt once said, "Anyone with visions should see a doctor," realistic ideas about the future are an essential feature of running a company. A vision provides a clear direction and shows a picture of the future that is better than the status quo. It is the starting point for change within the company.

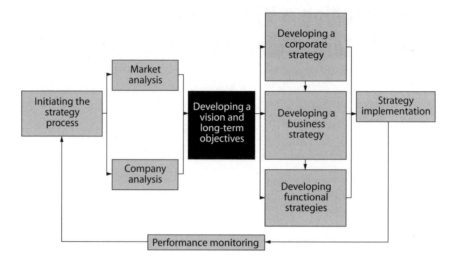

Figure 6.1: Developing a vision and long-term objectives as the fifth stage of the process

What features should a vision have?

Processes of change are painful. Employees must break out of their usual routine and learn new skills, do without resources, or live with the risk of their working conditions being radically changed. The vision should motivate the workforce to cope with these strains. It must be possible to translate the general vision of the future into long-term company objectives, and apply them to each employee's area. If, for example, one part of the company vision is to improve the professionalism of project management, then individual employees should try to interpret this general vision for themselves: "How do I manage projects? What does professionalism mean in my field? What systems, resources, and knowledge must be built up to close the current gaps?" These and other questions help to give meaning to the vision, but, unfortunately, in most companies too little time is spent working on the company vision and interpreting it for their own workforce. Employees are generally motivated if they can clearly see their own contribution to the overall success.

Use the vision as a superior tool for coordination

A vision can help to provide coordination vertically (through the levels of the hierarchy) and horizontally (across the functions). The budgeting process at the end of the year contributes to orienting the whole organization towards a common three-year target, and therefore to a common vision. Unfortunately, budget rounds often deal only with resources, and employ a few cunning tricks to defend last year's input. Output orientation would be desirable, as would a true interpretation and discussion of the figures on the table. In order to achieve this, it may be sensible to carry out the first round of target-setting without any figures, with purely qualitative information that is not backed up by figures until the second round. If strategies for achieving targets are developed at departmental, functional, or group level, the overall vision will provide the criteria for the choice of alternatives.

Master the balancing act between flexibility and stability

While long-term objectives refer to a three-year period, a vision should go beyond this. Visions too should be given a date. At the beginning of the 1990s, Ciba-Geigy drew up the vision Ciba 2000. In the current period of instability, many companies find it hard to draw up such visions. As a reaction, they either become set on global objectives, which results in the vision becoming dull and losing its significance, or they give up on it completely. However, in most companies you will find themes that have determined their development in the past. These themes may not be to do with the marketplace, but with their own capabilities and resources. Instead of beginning by asking what customer requirements should be met by which products and services, companies could consider which capabilities and resources they want to develop in the future. This way of proceeding is the core statement of the resource-based strategic approach, which is based on the assumption that the future direction comes not from outside but from within.

Create a picture of the future that is attractive and feasible for all interest groups

The vision can describe all the components examined by a SWOT analysis. The aim is that all interest groups should be able to identify with the vision. It can take as much account of investors, owners, and employees as the state or environmental organizations. But the vision should not degenerate into a mere PR instrument consisting only of fine phrases about a glorious future, but should treat the expectations of the interest groups in a concrete way. The groups involved should also perceive the vision as feasible. Of course it should set challenging targets, but it must be clear that there are practicable ways of achieving them within the desired period of time. If the interest groups are to appreciate the vision, it must be easy to communicate. Michael Eisner, the CEO of Walt Disney, is convinced that an idea is good if it can be explained in a few key sentences and still be inspiring. See whether you can write your vision on a beer mat.

Leadership in the strategy process

Leadership includes developing a vision for other people, who can be convinced by it to follow the leader. If you look for successful leaders in the past, you find an enormous variety of different types: fat and thin, democratic and dictatorial, women and men, with and without charisma, choleric and coolly calculating. The success of styles of leadership is very dependent on the context in which the leaders find themselves. In the various phases of development (foundation, growth, maturity, and restructuring), the company needs different leading personalities. Perhaps you have once been asked in a workshop to work out the adjectives to describe the best and worst boss. The outcome is reassuring: Good bosses must be supermen or superwomen: good communicators, good listeners, analytical thinkers, visionaries...You will probably get an exhaustive list of all the positive qualities from the evaluation records of your personnel department.

Top-down or bottom-up leadership? Do the spaghetti test

Next time you have spaghetti, before you cook it, take out a string of spaghetti and try to push it from one end of the table to the other with your finger. With a bit of skill, you will probably manage it. Now do the same experiment with a string of cooked spaghetti. There is nothing you can do except pick it up between two fingers and pull it from the front. Companies function in a similar way. If things are going well, it can be run from behind. That is the positive interpretation of "empowerment" – the employees actually know best what they have to do, and managers try to support them as best they know how. A few firms even have inverted organization charts, with the top management where the manual workers are usually to be found. This is known as "the inverted organization."

However, as soon as things are not going so well for the organization and the "cooked" spaghetti (without direction or self-motivation) is hanging from the chairs, you need real powers of leadership, managers who know their sphere of influence and use it consistently. This is called "leading from the front." In such uncertain situations, initiatives to take things in hand are important. It is probably even better to go a bit beyond your own competences. Bold leaders mostly prefer to ask for forgiveness afterwards, rather than seek permission from countless people beforehand. The harsh reality is, unfortunately, that usually only a very few people are prepared to take responsibility and make their presence felt. As in a poor game of soccer, they pass the ball to someone else as quickly as possible.

Motivation: Theories X, Y, Z...

Over the years, three different basic assumptions have been made about the motivation structure of people in the world of work.

Theory X. Managers have a duty to organize and monitor the work of their subordinate employees, because the latter are basically passive, unambitious, lazy, and opposed to change.

Theory Y. Managers must create the kind of conditions within the organization that allow self-motivated employees to give of their best.

Theory Z. Above all, managers must structure human relations and working conditions in a way that makes the employees feel good. If they do, most employees' self-esteem and productivity will rise. In this mixture of American and Japanese leadership styles, the manager thinks of the importance of the human component in the organization and emphasizes the organization's philosophy and culture.

From this and a large number of other motivation theories, managers can draw the conclusion that each individual employee needs to be motivated in a different way. Motivation by reward, punishment, job rotation, job enrichment, or other measures for structuring work and the working environment must be tailored to fit. Tips intended to suit everyone have no place here.

Develop your own principle of success for effective leadership in the strategy process

Successful leadership depends on the right interaction between the environment and the leading personality. There are probably no patent recipes that will help in all situations. All the same, from the mass of management literature you can get a general indication of what makes a successful manager.

Select your area of activity carefully. In order to achieve a good performance, you must choose an area of activity that you enjoy. This applies equally to both employees and management.

Distinguish between a career as a specialist and a career as a leader. Not all gifted people are also good leaders. You can probably learn to lead others to a certain extent. But why should the best engineer necessarily head the department? In a management position, expert knowledge fades into the background, and social and conceptual skills become more important. Pass on your skills to your staff and be proud if they become better than you in their specialist area. A leader must take over the function willingly, and approach interacting with other people with a certain measure of self-confidence and energy.

Choose your staff carefully. The choice, promotion, and correct use of employees to fit into the team are important tasks for managers. Only with a strong team can you produce exceptional performance. Irrespective of how well you manage your team, with a mediocre team you will achieve only average results. So you must be prepared to move or fire workers.

Stand by your decisions. Allow yourself enough time to prepare for decisions, but once you have decided, only really radically new information should justify a reevaluation. Continual questioning of decisions can lead to a culture of indecision, and paralyze the company.

Create a productive working environment. Create an infrastructure and a working environment in which high performance is possible. Sometimes you must budget creatively in order to do this, perhaps to replace the old computer that takes 15 minutes to boot up. Pay particular attention to the layout of the office. Just moving a group to a different floor or the other side of a corridor can make a big difference to communication.

Define what you mean by success. Make it clear to your workforce what success is, how it should be measured, and not least who is the judge of success. Do this test: Every employee should be able, without too much time to think, to answer the question of what the five most important success figures are. When do you open a bottle of champagne with your group at the end of the year and celebrate an exceptionally successful year? Do you also communicate to those around you that success is not due to them alone, but that team leadership is behind it?

Take care of strategically important projects yourself. In the long run, managers who only delegate and never work in the front line lose credibility. The last thing your employees want are bosses who put themselves in the foreground to take the praise for other people's successful projects, but shirk their responsibilities when it comes to mistakes and point the finger at others. It is still true to say that setting an example is a crucial part of a manager's daily work.

How are strategic alternatives assessed and selected?

The vision and the long-term objectives form the basis for the selection of strategic alternatives. Process fairness is created by defining criteria and the procedure for selecting strategic alternatives before they are even drawn up. This way of proceeding may contribute to the fact that, although the members of a decision-making body may not be 100 per-cent happy with the content of the decision, they still feel that the decision-making process was fair and therefore accept the decision. It is very unlikely that a clearly "correct" strategy can be separated from the "wrong" approaches purely by logical and objective thinking. Every strategy has its advantages and disadvantages, and approval of one strategy or the other is very much dependent on the individual manager's interests. That is why compromises reflecting the current power structure are often reached when choosing a strategy. So always establish the rules for choosing strategic alternatives before these alternatives are drawn up.

Make your strategy visible

One basic prerequisite for the choice of strategies is that they should be clearly visible: "Our strategy is to achieve profitable growth in our markets by targeting the way we address our customers' needs." Does this sentence contain a statement about the company strategy? Hardly. This general statement also applies to most firms, and therefore cannot be challenged. However, it does not say anything about the firm's current situation. These empty words are worse that remaining silent, as they leave the company believing it has a strategy. The same goes for the intuition of individuals. If their feelings are not explicitly stated, the strategy cannot be tested. In addition, coordinating the implementa-tion of a strategy is made harder, because the employees do not have a basic understanding of strategic action. Making a strategy visible does not necessarily mean producing 250 PowerPoint slides or writing a long business plan. A strategy can also be made clear to the company through concrete actions and spreading the message of the success of some of the implementation projects.

Use the principles of military strategy

For a large number of companies, military principles of warfare can be used when assessing strategic alternatives (see Pümpin 1980; von Oetinger, von Ghyczy, and Bassford 2001). The following questions test the suitability of a strategy.

1. *Are our forces being used in a concentrated way?* This tests whether, with the chosen strategy, the company's resources are not being wasted on too many departments or projects. In addition, attention is directed to whether the strategy is contributing to the targeted buildup of a few competitive advantages.

2. *Does the strategy build on our strengths?* Only in exceptional cases should the company try to spend most of its energy in correcting its weaknesses. If possible, the weaknesses should be avoided and only the strengths be brought to the fore. As already discussed in the section on SWOT analysis, the main attention should be directed towards areas where a strength coincides with a market opportunity. The second priority should be to discuss how far the strategy contributes to warding off threats from outside that coincide with a weakness.

3. *Does the strategy include innovative components?* In the end, higher profits can only be achieved through innovation. Product innovations can lead to greater differentiation, which in turn can cut down on extra charges. Process innovations mostly lead to lowering the costs of production and other value-creating activities, thus also increasing profit margins.

4. *Does the strategy exploit synergy potential?* In military confrontations, it is seen as a matter of course that the individual units, such as artillery, infantry, air force, or logistics mutually support and complement one another. The commanders of each individual unit do not need to be urged to cooperate, as they have a common goal: to win the battle and survive. In a company with a number of departments, this is not always the case. Although the German television stations Pro7 and Sat 1 are united under one company roof, the management of Pro7 is always delighted when it gets a

higher share of viewers than Sat 1 (and no doubt vice versa). On the one hand, this internal competition can spur both teams on to keep on improving. On the other hand, a strategy should consciously make use of all the "weapons" inside a group, if this is considered sensible. Working out a common target (and the corresponding internal cost calculation) is particularly important here. Synergy potentials can also be found in the company's external cooperation network.

5. *Is the risk involved in the strategy reasonable?* A strategy is always accompanied by some degree of uncertainty. Especially in the media sector, we can see how media moguls like Rupert Murdoch or Leo Kirch put their companies at stake for risky projects (and sometimes lose). For good reasons, investment advisers point out that investments in shares should be made using money that will not be required at short notice. That is why the risk in the investment mix of private investors decreases in proportion to their increasing age. Only if they have sufficient reserves available can private individuals decide to accept a higher degree of risk. In the case of particularly risky projects such as movie production, a movie studio may form a consortium with its competitors in order to share both the risk and the profits.

6. *Is the strategy clear and simply constructed?* If the strategy is too complex, communicating and implementing it becomes too difficult. In the Swiss army, the complexity of the strategy is adapted to the level of leadership. The leaders of squads of infantry command their soldiers using simple three-point orders: "Target – Way to the target – Conduct at the target." One step higher up, the platoon commanders assemble their squad leaders and use five-point orders. They often build a model of the terrain in the forest, using twigs, stones, and moss, on which they can demonstrate visually how the battle plan looks. A simple strategy is also important, because, as it gets more complex, it becomes increasingly difficult to build up an effective and manageable organizational structure.

Choose the strategy that promises the biggest discounted cashflow

Another possible approach to choosing alternative strategies is, as with easily definable investment projects, to predict the future cashflow and add it to the average discounted capital costs. This is a matter of discounted cashflow. The influence of each strategic alternative should be considered using this procedure. In the case of plans involving a higher degree of risk, you should calculate using higher capital costs. However, this analytical procedure can entail the risk of apparent accuracy. Strategies are much more complex than individual investment projects, and provide a general guideline for the future development of the company. It is therefore difficult to make cashflow predictions several years ahead.

Of course, it would be nice if we could predict precisely what influence strategy version A would have on the firm's profits, but in practice such attempts have proved illusory. Business plans that consist of 70 percent budget and other figures but few qualitative statements should be read with some care. We recommend always to include a qualitative approach to the evaluation of strategies. Identify the factors that will influence profits in the long term. Choose the strategy that promises the greatest chance of having a positive effect on these factors, even if this influence can only be quantified to a limited extent (Figure 6.2).

Assess the feasibility of the strategy

Next, you should assess the alternative strategies, so as to examine whether the organizational changes required by the implementation of the strategy are justifiable. The principle of "Structure follows strategy" (Chandler 1962) – that is, the strategy determines the choice of organizational structure – is usually correct, but some reservations must be noted. If the company has been through a big reorganization in the last year, the employees need a period of calm. Another phase of restructuring would make people feel unsure and seriously impair the efficiency of processes. In such cases, "Strategy follows structure" or even "Strategy follows IT" apply (if important company processes are strongly supported by information technology).

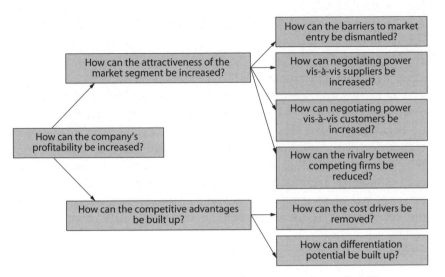

Figure 6.2: Influence of the strategy on the company's profitability

A further point to examine is whether the company's internal resources are sufficient to implement the strategy successfully. As well as the financial means, the employees' expert knowledge and the company culture must be considered. It is very unlikely, for example, that the majority of Italian postal workers would develop a culture of customer orientation, punctuality, and reliability within two to three years. Often the market image is a barrier to the implementation of the strategy. Some 70–80 percent of Italian students regularly raise their hands, when asked which of them has ever used the unreliability of the Italian mail as an excuse for letters they have not sent.

So the strategy should pick up on market trends and target opportunities for growth. The data presented are based on an analysis of the most important market factors, and its reliability must be tested. In addition, it is important to work out early-warning indicators that can show whether the firm is actually on the right path and if the strategy adopted is working.

The contribution made by developing a vision and long-term objectives within the framework of the strategic process: The objectives are clear, and so are the criteria for selecting the version of the strategy. You have now got as far as defining the way to the goal. This occurs at three strategic levels: corporate

strategy, business strategy, and functional strategy. If you have done everything correctly, your objectives and visions are defined in such a way that the participants in the strategy process are themselves capable of drawing up a strategy for the vision and implementing it in a logical way. Try to limit your strategy to a comparatively small area over which you have influence, rather than planning a "big hit."

7. Developing a Corporate Strategy

What you need to do when developing a corporate strategy (Figure 7.1): Before you develop a strategy, you should think about the general role of the company headquarters. In many cases, the company headquarters actually destroys value, either because it has no understanding of the markets in which the individual business units operate or because it does not have at its disposal resources that complement those available to the departments. Basically, the company headquarters should make it its task to develop synergies, allocate (financial) resources, plan globalization and diversification policies, and take responsibility for performance monitoring and the coaching of management at business unit level.

On close examination, it unfortunately becomes clear that the company headquarters often hinders rather than helps individual business units in their quest for success. In many instances, the company headquarters is very large and therefore costly. Ill-considered acquisitions, bad appointments, rash interventions in the operations of subsidiaries, or ineffective control mechanisms may result in the destruction rather than the creation of value. Why are most business unit managers not overjoyed when someone from the company headquarters comes on a visit? Admittedly, the vanity of not allowing one's decision-making to be influenced by others plays a part. Often, however, employees at business unit level do not regard the visit as an offer of concrete assistance, but rather as an attempt to exert control with little if any knowledge of the market in question. To put it more harshly, even if the representatives of the company headquarters were to work for nothing, they would still destroy shareholder value.

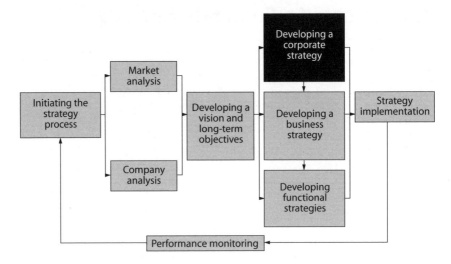

Figure 7.1: Developing a corporate strategy as the sixth stage of the process

Promote entrepreneurship in subsidiaries

The mere existence of a company headquarters often gives rise to a negative psychological consequence at the business unit level, with employees relying on the company headquarters to bail them out if market success eludes them. Entrepreneurs become managers dedicated, in the best-case scenario, to operating the business unit in the interests of group management, rather than battling it out in the front line for market success and hence survival. The declarations of success that frequently follow in the wake of demergers or management buyouts suggest that, in many groups, the headquarters creates little value and may even have a negative effect. If you've seen the movie *Pretty Woman*, you will know how the investor played by Richard Gere buys up large companies in order to break them up into smaller units and sell them off. The value of the parts thus disposed of is far greater than the price paid for the entire company. Thanks to these mostly highly leveraged acquisitions and the failure of the company headquarters, he is well able to afford the luxurious lifestyle he enjoys in the movie.

Define the role of the company headquarters

For these reasons, a corporate strategy should be approached with a great deal of caution and skepticism. The factors depicted in the matrix diagram in Figure 7.2 will help the company headquarters to reflect on its relationship with individual business units. Just try to position your business units within the matrix. How well do you understand the principles animating their activities and the market mechanisms they have to contend with? Which of their resources or capabilities might be strengthened with assistance from the company headquarters?

If you have a business unit located in the first quadrant, you should ask yourself whether it might not generate more value in another group of companies, and should therefore be disposed of. If this business unit is not to be sold, then it is better to manage it as a financial holding and refrain as far as possible from influencing its management decisions.

If you understand the business well but have nothing to offer, then ballast has been generated. The company headquarters should try to convert this ballast as quickly as possible into complementary resources and capabilities for the business units. A company headquarters with excellent engineers, who understand the business logic wonderfully well, will contribute little to the business units' success if good

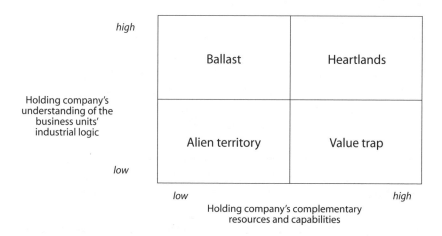

Figure 7.2: Holding company's contribution to departmental competitiveness (after Campbell and Goold 1998)

engineers are also employed in those business units. This dead weight should be replaced as quickly as possibly by marketing experts, for example.

A company may fall into the value trap if a business unit is lacking marketing experts, for instance, and the marketing division at central level uses successful ideas from other industries without adapting them. Business units in the "heartlands" benefit from group resources. However, it is still worth checking whether it would not be more sensible to develop these resources and capabilities at business unit level, or even to source them in the external market. In the "heartlands" quadrant, the company headquarters basically has four areas of responsibility.

Redistribution of resources. The resources generated by business operations are reinvested in the individual business units. This is usually done on the basis of an analysis of market attractiveness (size, growth, or other factors). Analyses of this kind may lead to internationalization, diversification, or disinvestment.

Monitoring and coaching of business units. The business unit strategy is developed in collaboration with the company headquarters, or at least given its blessing. The business units' performance is monitored from time to time in the course of the year, and measures may be introduced if targets are not met. The level of intervention depends very much on the company headquarters' understanding of its role and on the business units' situation. If all the business units in a group are functioning successfully and autonomously, the center can limit itself to appointing the top managers and approving the annual financial statement. In crisis situations, on the other hand, the business unit management may need to liaise weekly with the company headquarters about the measures taken. It may even be necessary temporarily to centralize decision-making in order to introduce important processes of change.

Creation of synergies. The experience of many groups shows that efforts to create synergies must be initiated by the company headquarters. Since business units within a group compete with each other for resources, willingness to cooperate is not usually granted spontaneously. Thus, it is the company headquarters' task to urge the business units to cooperate. In many cases, the company headquarters has taken up the cause of developing group-wide competences and a shared culture, for which the effective implementation of initiatives is more important than setting a strategic orientation.

Communication with external interest groups. The public profile of a company headquarters depends very much on its own understanding of its role. The center frequently takes responsibility for communicating with banks, investors, or other interest groups in order to ensure the consistency of company statements and to maximize its influence.

How are synergies created?

Synergy is actually management doublespeak. There is much talk of synergies, particularly when mergers are announced. You'll certainly have heard the formula 2 + 2 = 5 being used to explain the notion of synergy. Investment banks have taken up the idea, and give a generous assessment to potential buyers of the value of the synergies that might be achieved. If a deal goes ahead, however, managers are often faced with the sobering realization that synergies are in fact difficult to achieve. The notion of "horizontal strategies" (Porter 1980) was developed as a means of systematically evaluating synergies. Business units can be linked horizontally at three levels: the value chain and its associated activities; the transfer of know-how; and the coordination of strategies against common competitors.

Link activities in the value chain

Economies of scale, that is, reductions in unit costs, are achieved by increasing the output of a particular category of product. Economies of scope are achieved by improving the utilization of existing capacities through the coordination of several product categories. If a diversified firm succeeds in linking the value-creating activities of different business units without causing fixed costs to increase, then it can achieve cost advantages over nondiversified companies. Concrete examples are the shared use of distribution channels (cross-selling) or joint purchasing activities. It is important to focus on the cost drivers rather than attempting to coordinate marginal activities, since coordination costs can easily exceed the reductions in production costs. Economies of scale and scope are particularly important in industries and stages of the value chain that have a high share of fixed costs that cannot be reduced by outsourcing.

Economies of scope not only produce cost advantages, but can also give rise to differentiation advantages for firms. Examples of this include the sale of several products from one source, product improvements through internal benchmarking (Barney 2001), or joint R&D activities. One awkward but all-the-more-important aspect of activity coordination is internal invoicing for services between business units. Ways must be found of distributing costs when a member of the sales team suddenly has to place additional products from other business units, or the controlling division becomes responsible for several business units.

Coordinate the transfer of know-how

The transfer of knowledge and know-how from one business unit to another is a further way for diversified companies to achieve competitive advantages. The methods that can be used to promote such transfers were outlined in Chapter 5. One example of the difficulties that can arise with the transfer of know-how is the coordination of international exchanges between national companies and their company headquarters. Various role models for national companies are outlined below, depending on how much knowledge is contributed and received by the group (Gupta and Govindarajan 1991).

Local innovators. A national company contributes little relevant know-how to other parts of the group but, on the other hand, makes scarcely any use of know-how from within the group either. Consequently, no synergies are created by exchanges of know-how. This may be reasonable if the national company is a purely financial investment or if a germ cell of new know-how and activity is deliberately to be built up without regard for existing activity.

Contributors. If a national company contributes know-how of relevance to other parts of the group, but without using know-how generated elsewhere in the group, then synergies are achieved by one-sided exchanges of know-how. This makes sense when it seems advantageous to concentrate the development of know-how in one part of the company, and the know-how produced there can be easily disseminated throughout the company.

Implementers. Implementers make intensive use of the know-how generated by other parts of the company, but make very little contribution themselves to the general pool of knowledge and know-how. It would be a fallacy to believe that each national company should actively generate knowledge and know-how as a competence center in one area, in order subsequently to diffuse that know-how throughout the entire company. For example, national companies with very small turnovers may have purely operational functions, since it would be too expensive to invest time in the development of specific knowledge and know-how. For national companies that were stuck in command economies for decades, it may make sense to bring their know-how up to the level of the modern market economy over a lengthy period, without enforcing a demand for excellence in a particular area.

Integrated players. These national companies make intensive use of knowledge from other parts of the group, while at the same time contributing a great deal of knowledge for others to use. Companies in this category can be divided into two groups. Those in the first group, who might be termed knowledge brokers, see it as their task to identify sources of knowledge in any part of the company and to pass this knowledge on to other national companies. Those in the second group are more active, since they develop their own knowledge and make it available for others to use. At the same time, networked experts apply knowledge and know-how from other parts of the company to local problems.

Discuss with your management team which roles your individual subsidiaries are currently filling. On the basis of these discussions, assess whether individual national companies are correctly positioned. Then organize your knowledge-management systems in such a way that the desired position is supported as well as possible or can be achieved cost-effectively.

Coordinate your business unit strategies against
common competitors

A third element in a horizontal strategy is the coordination of business
unit strategies against common competitors. Fighting a common
"enemy" may motivate business unit managers to bite the bullet,
change their own return targets, and subordinate themselves to the
corporate strategy. For example, it may be necessary to attack competitors in their home market by introducing low prices in business
unit A, in order to protect business unit B in its own home market. If
business unit B produces substantially more sales and profits for the
company as a whole, then it may make sense to sacrifice margins in
business unit A so as to reduce the competitors' cashflow. In the long
term, however, the cross-subsidizing of business units is no solution for
strategic problems in particular business segments.

How are diversification processes managed?

Diversification is defined as the simultaneous buildup of new markets
and products. The matrix depicted in Figure 7.3 is often described as
the "growth matrix" and sets diversification alongside other possible
sources of business growth.

Greater market penetration should be sought if the market is not yet
fully saturated, the product's frequency of use can be increased, market
share can be easily won from the competition, the effect of advertising
on sales was strong in the past and is not yet fully exhausted, and
economies of scale can create additional competitive advantages.

Efforts should be made to develop in a new market, whether it be a
consumer or a geographical market, when:

● inexpensive, but reliable, new distribution channels can be used
● a successful formula can be transferred relatively easily to
  another market
● new markets exist that are either unexplored or unsaturated
● financial and human resources are available for the expansion
● surplus production capacities can be used

- strong trends can be detected towards globalization in the industry
- highly developed strategic and organizational capabilities make it possible quickly to develop a basic understanding of the new market.

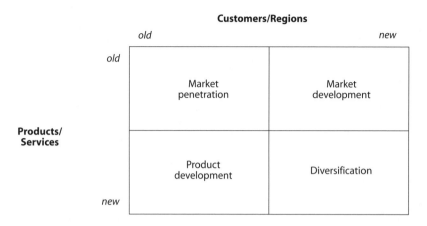

Figure 7.3: Growth matrix (Ansoff 1958)

It makes sense to try to develop a new product market when existing products are at the end of their life cycle, technological change is a driving force for change in an industry, the industry is in a saturation phase and it is becoming increasingly difficult to use differentiation advantages to achieve premium prices, and the company is better endowed with R&D capabilities than the average firm in the industry.

The general rule is that a company should first exhaust all the possibilities available to it to increase market penetration, and develop both markets and products, before it diversifies into new areas. If you have reached this stage, there are various measures that should be taken before the decision is made to diversify.

Evaluate the current portfolio

Before any consideration is given to possible diversifications of the business portfolio, you need to review its current state. There are two basic aspects to any assessment of a department. First, is it in an attractive industry? Second, does it have sufficient resources and capabilities to achieve competitive advantages? The so-called BCG matrix (named after the Boston Consulting Group) is probably the best-known portfolio matrix. A segment is classified as attractive if it has high market growth. Relative strength is assessed on the basis of one factor only, namely market share relative to that of the three largest competitors. General Electric, in collaboration with McKinsey, has further operationalized this factor. Thus, the first step in working with this matrix is to explore with the management team when a segment is attractive and how relative strength is to be measured. Build up your own company-specific portfolio matrix. Then position the departments, represented as circles of differing radii and colors, within the matrix; the radius of each circle could correspond to turnover, for example, and the color of the circle to the level of cashflow.

Interpretation of the BCG matrix is based on the position of each department in the portfolio. Four basic positions can be identified: question marks, stars, cash cows, and dogs. Just like products, business units also have a life cycle: New business units are established for a growing (attractive) market. If the company is a pioneer, the business unit may be relatively strong from the outset. In many cases, however, others are already operating in the market, and initially the company is in the question-mark position. Cashflows are usually strongly negative and management must set clear time limits, within which it has to be demonstrated that the market position can be significantly improved and the attractiveness of the market is a long-term trend and not a passing fad. Stars are market leaders in attractive segments. Cashflow is usually neutral, since there is a considerable need for (re)investment in order to fund the growth.

Since only very few segments continue to grow over several decades, there is always, needless to say, a point at which a star mutates into a cash cow. Business units are described as cash cows when market attractiveness declines, but their own market share and relative strength remain high. Cashflows in such business units are strongly positive. This means that a highly selective and cautious approach is now taken to investment, in order to free up resources for more attractive markets. Low-growth markets usually give rise to a struggle among the established market participants to crowd out the competition. It becomes increasingly difficult for a company to use quality as a differentiating factor, since price becomes the number-one purchasing criterion, with cost competition becoming increasingly important as a result. This causes a business unit to slump from its position as a cash cow into the dog position. In such a case, only the most essential resources should be made available. A market-exit strategy might also be developed, to be implemented if efforts to give another boost to the market through new technologies or other radical innovations come to nothing. Market-exit strategies should be drawn up well ahead of time, because bailing out quickly can give rise to major problems (such as the need to draw up layoff programs, honor long-term benefit guarantees, or dispose of specialist equipment).

Give reasons why the company should diversify

Imagine you are the manager of a business unit that is a cash cow. Let us assume, moreover, that the company headquarters allocates resources strictly in accordance with the BCG matrix. As a result, money is siphoned off from your business unit. What arguments can you advance in order to tie those resources to your business unit? One important argument, surely, is that companies must have a balanced portfolio and that certain replacement investments need to be made in order to prevent the decline from cash cow to dog. Furthermore, positioning is heavily dependent on how the market segment is defined. Indeed, you can define it so narrowly that you become the market leader. Moreover, the portfolio matrix is an attempt to give a two-dimensional depiction of reality, which in fact provides a distorted view. One final argument to clinch your critique of a strategy that relies solely on the BCG matrix is that it often ignores important synergy effects between cash cows and question marks.

Diversification means investing in new business units because the existing portfolio has insufficient presence in attractive markets. The portfolio matrix certainly provides some important information that can be used to explain why a company should diversify. However, decisions should not be taken solely on this basis. Diversification must be well founded, and the justification differs depending on the nature of the diversification. Empirical studies have shown that diversification tends to be more successful if it is targeted at adjoining segments. In the 1970s, many conglomerates were formed in the general growth euphoria that prevailed at that time, only to come under considerable pressure 20 years later. In the 1990s, therefore, the watchword was "Back to core competences." Firms began to limit themselves again to what they could do well and to the markets they understood.

However, there are also reasons for diversifying into unrelated markets. They include cashflow management, long-term reorientation in a more attractive area, tax optimization, or a chance to acquire an undervalued company. Minimizing risk across the entire portfolio is often advanced as a reason by management. This argument probably applies principally to managements seeking to safeguard their jobs in the long term. For a company's owners, however, there are simpler ways of balancing risks through the international capital markets.

Companies diversifying into related markets often give synergies in value-creation activities as the reason. Joint R&D, complementary distribution channels, and more efficient production are just a few examples. If diversification is to be successfully implemented, it is important to be clear in advance about such synergies, to assess them realistically (and evaluate them financially), and to formulate a plan for taking advantage of them consistently in day-to-day business operations.

Determine the direction of diversification

The decision as to what direction a company seeking to diversify should take depends heavily on the structure of the market in question (market power and economies of scale and scope) and on the attitude of top management (willingness to take risks and expectations of growth and profit). Companies wishing to diversify can take one of four different directions.

1. *Vertical diversification.* Strengthen control and involvement in upstream or downstream stages of the industry's value chain. Firms adopting a vertical diversification strategy can go either forward (into distribution channels) or backward (towards suppliers). Forward integration is appropriate when the following conditions are met.

   a. Distribution channels are unreliable or expensive, or do not meet requirements in other respects.

   b. There are no competent sales and distribution partners.

   c. The company has the resources and capabilities to build up a distribution channel itself.

   d. Growth in the market segment will continue to be stable in future (forward integration reduces the capacity for disinvestment).

   e. There are considerable advantages for production in having a readily quantifiable sales volume.

   f. The profit margin in the current distribution channels is (too) high.

2. *Horizontal diversification.* A company invests in complementary or even substitute products for existing customers. Thus, carmakers frequently offer financial or insurance products to car buyers. Horizontal diversification can lead to a firm building up a virtually monopolistic market position without being called to account by the antitrust authorities.

3. *Concentric diversification.* Core competences constitute the starting point for concentric diversification. These existing competences are used to develop new products in new markets. For example, plant engineering and construction companies can use extruder technology to produce plant and equipment for food processing or the manufacture of pharmaceuticals. Concentric diversification can also refer to a situation in which management capabilities are transferred from one industry to another. In concentric diversification, it is important that the capabilities on which the new market and product development is based really do have the potential to cause difficulties for existing competitors.

4. *Conglomerates.* The new business units have no points of contact with the existing ones. Since many conglomerates were not successful in the past, many tenuous links with the existing business are invented. That is why certain questions are increasingly being asked: "What exactly are related business units? How can this be measured? Is it sufficient to have transferable general rules in order to deal satisfactorily with forces in the industry?" It would seem more sensible to accept diversification into unrelated business units for what it is, and to manage the new business units as relatively separate entities.

Define the mode of diversification

Figure 7.4 summarizes the various forms of market entry for you. At the first level, a distinction is made between modes of entry with and without equity investment. Generally speaking, equity investments are advantageous when management is seeking a high degree of control over its diversification strategy. However, the price of such control is often exposure to greater financial risk. National authorities sometimes insist that foreign firms take minority holdings in joint ventures. If such constraints do not exist, managers will adjust the need for control to the risks and business conditions that exist in the country in question, as will be discussed in detail at a later stage.

Basically, a distinction can be made between two forms of development: internal and external. Both modes of diversification have advantages and disadvantages, with which managers ought to be familiar.

- The term "intrapreneurship" is often used when new business units are developed internally; it denotes the implementation of entrepreneurial ideas using a company's own resources. It is often worth while setting up a new, legally independent organization (spin-off), in order to limit the risk in the event of failure, on the one hand, and, on the other, to restrict the restraining influence of those units

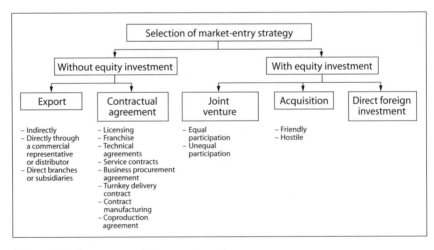

Figure 7.4: Summary of forms of market entry

already in existence. So-called internal venture-capital units can accelerate this process. Although internal development is often slower, and a great deal of time is taken to build up new resources and capabilities, it usually produces outcomes that are more compatible with the existing company culture. There are also fewer of the transaction costs incurred in integrating old and new business processes.

- Companies opting for external development have a choice between mergers and acquisitions, joint ventures, or other forms of strategic alliances. External development can be quicker, turn possible competitors into partners or eliminate them through acquisition, and provide access to additional resources. However, the costs of acquisitions are often considerable, and unwanted parts of the company must be included in the purchase. Moreover, attempts to integrate different companies always bring cultural complications with them.

- Strategic alliance is a general term for various forms of cooperation, such as joint ventures, franchises, equity participation, or other long-term contractual links that help to expand the business. The aim of strategic alliances is to avoid the disadvantages of acquisitions, while at the same time providing a basis for developing a new business area quickly. They are a way of circumventing the need to purchase those parts of a company that are of no interest. At the same time, however, there is less scope for exerting control. It pays to check carefully whether an alliance is really a strategic one.

Identify, evaluate, and select your targets

Once the direction and mode of diversification have been determined, actual targets (takeover candidates, cooperation partners, new markets) can be identified. The following three tests will help you assess the prospects for success.

1. *The market attractiveness test.* The industries and market segments picked out by an expanding firm should be structurally attractive.

2. *The market-entry cost test.* The costs of developing the new business area should not exceed the current value of the future profits. Find out how much it will cost to overcome the barriers to market entry.

Moreover, the market-entry costs are dependent on the speed and mode of market development.

3. *The synergy test.* Ask yourself why two business units that are being brought together as a result of diversification should be worth more together than each business unit by itself. Quantify the opportunities for coordinating activities between business units, and exchanging knowledge and know-how. And consider how well you understand and will be able to deal with the rules of competition in the new market.

Settle the transaction and integrate the new business unit

For most external transactions, you will call on an investment bank for professional assistance. However, make sure you use the bank not as a source of ideas but primarily as a partner in implementing your strategy. It is important that you begin to draw up an integration plan before the contract is signed, that is, in the due diligence phase. The most important staffing decisions should be taken and put into practice as soon as possible after the transaction is announced. The nature of the integration process depends on the new business unit's need to develop synergies with the existing business units and the state of its own business processes. On the basis of these two factors, four different forms of integration can be identified.

Financial holding company. If the business unit to be incorporated is a properly functioning one operating in an unrelated market and, consequently, having little if any potential for synergy, the company headquarters should interfere as little as possible in management decisions. The business unit should be managed principally by means of financial control mechanisms.

Management holding company. If the new business unit is in need of restructuring, the company headquarters can intervene directly in the decision-making processes as the management holding company, without affecting the existing business units. This approach should be adopted when the new business unit has only tenuous links with the rest of the group or only slight potential for synergy.

Absorption. In the case of an unsuccessful business unit that management regards as having considerable potential for synergy, its resources and processes should be taken apart and incorporated into the existing resources and processes. Once this has been done, there will be few traces of the acquisition left.

Symbiosis. In this case, the best resources and processes of both business units are identified and combined equally with each other.

How are internationalization processes managed?

Entry into new geographical markets is an increasingly important aspect of diversification. The pressure to globalize comes from various directions: technological innovation, increasingly global competitors, deregulation, reduction of trade restrictions, mobility of capital and other resources, high R&D costs, exploitation of lower cost factors in other countries, or simply the need for the best workers to operate in an international environment. Managers must understand that international diversification can involve not just the sale of products or services, but the totality of a company's activities. From this point of view, therefore, most companies are already operating internationally, even if they only recruit internationally, for example. Internationalization means giving thought to the mode, timing, and speed of market entry as well as to the selection of the new geographical market. Decisions must also be taken with regard to the organizational integration of the national companies.

Select your mode of market entry

Managers select the mode of market entry on the basis of two core factors: risk and the need for control. The risks of international diversification lie in different legal systems and business practices, which can cause difficulties for firms operating in foreign countries, as well as in the more obvious linguistic differences. Some of these risks can be evened out by investing in control instruments. International diversification strategies often begin with the export of products, either directly or indirectly through a local importer. If transportation costs are high, license agreements can be concluded with local companies; such agreements protect property rights. If the product succeeds in the market, a company can strengthen its presence by appointing local commercial agents. As sales increase, it may be worth while setting up a subsidiary with responsibility in the first instance for sales and customer care. As the operation expands, the subsidiary could take on additional functions, such as R&D, production, or procurement.

Select your geographical territory

Generally speaking, a company selects a market similar to its own in cultural, socioeconomic, and linguistic terms. Another obvious rule of thumb is that one should look first at markets in which the intensity of competition is still low, and growth and volumes are high. A foreign firm has to struggle with many barriers to entry, and local competitors are often able deliberately to exploit their home advantage. A multi-national company needs to offset these disadvantages with other advantages. Such advantages might be found in brand names, production efficiencies, or economies of scale and scope. It is important that multinational companies take care to identify the resources and capabilities that facilitate market entry, in order to choose their markets accordingly.

Decide on the timing of any expansion abroad

You will know from the discussion of the Ansoff matrix that you should not be thinking of extending your operations internationally until you have fully exhausted the opportunities offered by the home market. Managers are frequently prey to illusions about the rapid profits to be made abroad. In the first instance, however, any expansion into foreign markets means investing heavily for several years – and it is better if that takes place on a sound financial basis. Apart from these general statements about the timing of any expansion abroad, specific events may trigger an entry into foreign markets.

- When a competitor enters your market, you can try to attack your rival's cashflow in their home market.
- If there are substantial economies of scale to be achieved in certain industries, then it is sometimes necessary to operate internationally in order to realize them fully.
- Internationalization would be an option when critical resources and capabilities cannot be developed in the home market, or if the cost of doing so is too high.
- If demand for the company's products rises abroad or the domestic market is saturated, an entry into foreign markets suggests itself.
- Expansion abroad often takes place for personal reasons (the company owner meets an Indian industrialist at a golf tournament, and both discover they have interests in common).
- Decisions to go international are sometimes motivated by state subsidies and tax breaks.
- If its customers decide to operate internationally, a company may be forced to increase its global presence.

Determine the pace of the internationalization process

The pace of the internationalization process depends on both internal and external factors. Internal factors that might inhibit international growth are often financial in nature. However, financial resources can be procured relatively quickly. Consequently, it is the availability of skilled personnel, or the speed at which a suitable team can be assembled, that is usually the biggest challenge.

Company growth processes are often determined by a push-pull effect, both elements of which impact on the company's workforce.

Pull effect. If a team is newly formed, its work is hampered by considerable inefficiencies, with the result that more workers are required to complete a task than is the case with a more experienced team. Consequently, the speed at which team competences can be developed determines the company's possible growth rate.

Push effect. On the other hand, experienced teams are in a position to complete activities more efficiently and, hence, more quickly. The resulting surplus capacity can be a driver for further growth, for example, through diversification into international markets.

The external factors that can influence growth need to be considered in relation to the company's existing capabilities. The more similar the capabilities required for diversification are, the more quickly the diversification process can be driven forward. Of course, certain competences can be acquired in the market. However, the more novel they are, the longer they will take to integrate into the existing ones. External factors such as market growth, competition, or other structural characteristics of the industry in question also influence the growth process.

Define how the foreign subsidiaries are to be integrated into the organization

The integration of the foreign subsidiaries into the existing organizational structures begins with the restructuring of the company headquarters. One of the following organizational models could be adopted, depending on the complexity of the product and the level of turnover to be achieved abroad.

International division. If the product is not complex and turnover is low compared with the domestic market, an additional box is added to the existing organization chart, which accounts for the international activities.

Global products division. If a large number of different products are to be sold internationally, the group organization chart should be structured by product category.

Country organization. If product diversity is low and turnover in international markets is high, the organization chart should be structured by geographical region.

Matrix organization. The matrix organizational form is used when product diversity is great and the share of international sales high. The basic idea behind the matrix structure is to cushion the resultant complexity of the managerial environment by means of a large number of vertical and horizontal integration mechanisms. However, the matrix structure is probably the most controversial structure for companies operating internationally, since it is usually associated with high coordination costs. We suggest that one or other of the two organizational dimensions (products or countries) should take priority in decision-making processes.

The four organizational structures described above are ideal types. In practice, however, hybrid forms that have emerged as a result of the history of industrialization and political intrigue are common. It is very important that the management team in each national company has clearly defined contacts at the company headquarters, who represent their interests.

If possible, the organizational structures, systems, and processes should be replicated in the global organization. In other words, controlling or sales management systems should not differ from country to country. Moreover, individual national organizations can be allocated the role of competence centers if they have developed above-average capabilities in certain areas.

Determine the foreign subsidiaries' decision-making authority

One of the important responsibilities of an international manager is to determine the extent to which local companies should be free to take their own decisions. The two most important decision-making variables here are, on the one hand, the need for global standardization in order to be able to produce cost-effectively and, on the other, the necessary local adjustment to customer requirements in order to be able to stand out from the competition by virtue of product quality. In many matrix models, the "high-high quadrant" is the position to be reached. This does not apply to the matrix for local decision-making authority. Numerous examples have shown that the compromise between high global orientation and local adaptation does not necessarily produce the best results in the market.

Thus, depending on the degree of global integration and the need for local adjustment, four role models emerge (Bartlett and Ghoshal 1989).

Home-market-oriented implementer. This role model is frequently taken up by firms in the early stages of the internationalization process. All decisions are taken by the company headquarters, and the company's local representatives enjoy little, if any, autonomy. Market entry frequently comes about simply because another geographical region happens to respond positively to a product. However, the main focus of the product-development program continues to be the development of the best possible products for the domestic market.

Globally-oriented implementer. The role of the foreign subsidiary is still that of an implementer of decisions taken at central levels. In contrast to the home-market-oriented implementer, however, these decisions are not taken solely on the basis of domestic market data. The subsidiary is given the task of gathering local market information and passing it on to the parent company. The latter then tries to develop global solutions and products, which may represent a successful compromise for all the national companies.

Local kingdoms. If the company headquarters exerts little influence over local decisions, local kingdoms develop. A strongly entrepreneurial approach and proximity to local customers are the advantages of this role model. However, it is consciously accepted that these advantages are bought at the cost of global integration and the resulting synergies.

Distributed global competence centers. This compromise between the two axes has often been summarized by the motto "Think global – act local." In this model, local firms retain their decision-making autonomy, particularly in sales and customer service; at the same time, however, a policy of global integration is pursued in order to achieve economies of scale. In most cases, however, the push for global integration emanates not solely from company headquarters, but also from so-called competence centers. Local competences are identified and made systematically available to the other geographical territories.

The contribution made by developing a corporate strategy within the framework of the strategic process: You now know the

business areas in which you want to be active. Depending on how the company headquarters' role is defined, you have established the investment priorities for the various business units and are in a position to have well-founded discussions with all business unit managers about their strategies. You have a good idea of the most important management personnel in your group and you have planned how they are to be deployed. You clearly understand the value that is created at central level, and this is also acknowledged at business unit level.

8. Developing a Business Strategy

What you need to do when developing a business strategy (Figure 8.1): Bearing in mind the general demands laid down by the company headquarters, you must now decide how you are going to position yourself vis-à-vis the competition and your customers. Basically, you have a choice between a differentiation strategy, a cost-leadership strategy, and a focus strategy.

What distinguishes easyJet from British Airways? What strategy makes sense for PlayStation 2 when the Xbox comes onto the market? What options are open to small firms that large companies do not have? What links the German company Würth, a world leader in the supply of assembly materials, and Microsoft? Why, under certain circumstances, is it sensible to give products away? These are questions that companies in real-life competitive situations ask themselves. Our aim here is to support you as you develop strategies for new business units, scrutinize a company's current positioning, and try to operate in difficult competitive situations in a duly considered, well-founded way.

In essence, it's a matter of actively shaping the competition instead of being overrun by customers' expectations and competitors' strategies. And yet even at this early stage, the first note of caution must be sounded. If the teachings of a great deal of management theory are to be believed, it is better to be proactive than reactive. For this reason, a strategic orientation should be geared to the long term and should not be changed too frequently. Are "hot" strategies basically preferable to "lukewarm" strategies? Whatever these recommendations mean in essence, there is no doubt that the broad thrust of these statements is correct.

We start by outlining and analyzing basic types of strategies. Drawing on real-life examples, we will establish how different competitive strategies are defined and developed in the dynamic context of the

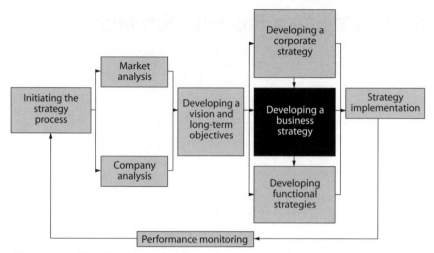

Figure 8.1: Developing a business strategy as the seventh stage of the process

market. On the one hand, it becomes clear that classification exercises of this kind are a useful tool, particularly since they also require firms to be consistent in their strategies. At the same time, however, it is striking how far the actual shaping of strategies is dependent on contingent factors, notably situation and position. Competitive strategies need to be considered in the context of different market phases. What makes sense in emerging markets, such as the Internet economy? How should companies behave in mature markets, like the so-called commodities (products characterized by a high degree of market and price transparency, for example, cement)? Are you an aggressor in a market seeking to win market share from the established players, or are you yourself defending a position?

What are the features of successful business strategies?

Time and time again, in the real world of business, we come across strategies that make us doubt the teachings of management theory.

Competitive strategies are the result of entrepreneurial calculation, changeable customer requirements, and competitors' and suppliers' strategies. Additionally, influences from the wider environment in which a department operates play a decisive role. Thus, the Phaeton, vw's luxury car, was designed for a target group made up of "upwardly mobile, individualistic, self-confident people." This is a target group that sounds very promising during periods of economic boom, such as that triggered by the miracle of the so-called new economy, but can be taken to absurd lengths during a period of recession.

In general, clear definitions of target groups or strategic market segments are the basis for competitive strategies, and are hence dependent on the changes that take place in markets. Another example that reveals the extent to which strategy is determined by the choice of market and its dynamic is the Smart car. Designed as a vehicle for the urban avant-garde, the car was initially a flop with precisely this target group. High-earning singles and childless dual-earner households, renting downtown apartments and having an open-minded, unconventional approach to life, were supposed to buy the Smart car as a second or third vehicle. In this way, the Smart car would have become a lifestyle product with a completely new approach to mobility. In reality, however, customers punished the marketing philosophers. The car has been taken up by a group of consumers who are using the vehicle's avant-garde image to enhance their own, considerably more conservative, image. The average purchaser of a Smart car is 42 years old, comfortably off, and male. So you see, markets change strategies, and strategies often have the opposite effect in markets to the one that was intended.

The competitive strategy should be the shaping force

An innovator's competitive advantage is important, since the first to enter a market can generally realize above-average returns. However, how sensible is it to copy? Does it not frequently make more sense to be the second in the market? Of course, Apple was the first into the newly created PC market with its superior Macintosh operating system. However, the company refused to grant licenses for its operating system to third-party producers. Today, the innovator Apple targets its system at an exclusive minority, while Microsoft has a quasi-monopoly over the market for PC operating systems.

A competitive strategy should function as a signal internally and externally

Average quality at average prices seldom leads to commercial success. And what about low prices with high additional utility? This sounds tempting: great design, decent quality, and low prices. That's ideal for customers and dangerous for suppliers. And yet, what is IKEA doing? Actually, IKEA offers average quality at moderate prices. In the overall strategic process, the business strategy is of fundamental and decisive importance, since it functions as the interface between planning and action. If, in planning our strategic positioning, we have opted for price leadership, this has direct consequences on product design, cost management, and marketing. Operational and functional arrangements are derived from a department's basic strategic orientation. In a way, its competitive strategy is a company's operational preprogramming.

Another reason why the competitive strategy is such a highly relevant element of the overall strategic process is its signaling function. The positioning of Mercedes as a leader in both quality and technology has great significance for customers, competitors, and employees. As well as the product itself, customers are buying the brand image. For competitors, Mercedes' positioning is of great significance for their own strategic orientation (demarcation/differentiation function). Thus, BMW, for example, emphasizes the sporty aspect of its car with the slogan "Sheer driving pleasure." And for employees in particular, a company's strategic positioning provides a clear signal that guides their work: cost or quality awareness as a maxim to act on. In this sense, the competitive strategy emerges as a company's cultural programming (genetic code).

Competitive strategies can often not be set aside

The positioning that ensues from a company's strategic decision-making cannot be easily reversed. There are only a few examples of companies that have succeeded in completely changing their basic strategic orientation. IBM may be one of them. Since the 1990s, the company has evolved from a hardware and technology company into a service provider. IBM bought up business consultancy firms, auditors, and information-technology service providers as well as massively reducing the share of its own production. It completely abandoned production of memory systems, for example. It is more financially rewarding for the company to provide services for information-technology products and systems, irrespective of the manufacturer, than to manufacture those products itself. IBM is now the largest service organization in the world. Nevertheless, it must be emphasized that fundamental strategic positions were not abandoned in the course of this transformation. IBM continues to rely on system solutions, and differentiates itself at various levels (technology, quality, image, customer service) from the competition. Other firms have failed miserably in the attempt to change their strategic positioning. Daimler-Benz, for example, failed in the attempts it made in the 1980s to develop from a carmaker into an integrated technology company.

The competitive strategy should be reliable and stable

A competitive strategy must be able to take hold in the market, and needs time to produce any payback. For customers and employees, a company's strategic positioning is an important signal associated with reliability, orientation, and, particularly, image. But how can long-term competitive advantages be gained by means of deliberate short-term changes of strategy? By adhering firmly to a particularly strategy, is there not a risk that a company will become predictable in the eyes of its competitors? And, in any case, how important to fickle customers is any one supplier's reliability?

It is quite right for firms to commit themselves to a basic strategic direction. Two basic types of strategy can be identified: cost leadership and differentiation (Porter 1980). The basic issue at stake here is that companies can survive in a competitive environment only if they have a clear competitive advantage over their rivals, and are able to maintain that advantage over the long term. Consequently, their position relative to their direct competitors is an important indicator of the success of their strategies. The question is how firms in a particular industry can secure relatively permanent advantages over their competitors through differentiation or cost reductions.

In adopting a cost-leadership strategy, a firm is trying to turn its superior cost control in the value-creation process into a competitive advantage. In a differentiation strategy, the competitive advantages are the result of value added, a unique additional utility that is offered to customers and for which they are prepared to pay a price premium. The additional utility may be better quality, unique service, or even a particular image. This competitive advantage is the reason why customers prefer one company's offer to that of its competitors. We will investigate in greater detail later how these strategies might be realized, and provide some examples of successful implementation and of the difficulties that might be encountered.

If a company is focused on just one subsegment of the market as a whole, then it is following a third type of strategy: a focus strategy, also known as a niche strategy. Having identified its niche, a company can pursue both cost-leadership and differentiation strategies. One industry that is characterized by niche suppliers is the machine-tool industry. The specialist provider of packaging machines for Italian panettone is far from being in a position to produce machines that meet the stringent requirements of the pharmaceutical industry. Here, too, there are specialists, such as packaging-machine manufacturers that have concentrated exclusively on blister packs and companies that are unbeatable in the production of collapsible tube packaging. As far as the niche for specialists in blister packs is concerned, there will be few competitors in this extremely narrow market segment that are able to operate as both cost leaders and differentiators. The consequences of this strategy are as follows.

● From the customers' point of view, highly specific requirements are optimally met by a very small number of suppliers.
● For firms, the market is manageable and coordination costs are low. Moreover, a company can generate considerable learning effects from specialization. However, dependency on one subsegment is associated with very high risk.
● For competitors operating outside the segment, the barriers to entry are high, because a considerable degree of specialization is required to service the market and meet customer requirements.

Thus, the difference lies in the scope of the target market. In a conventional cost-leadership or differentiation strategy the scope of the target market is very wide, whereas in a focus strategy the target market is very narrow and highly segmented.

How is a cost-leadership strategy developed?

A company that is a cost leader has succeeded in obtaining a competitive advantage by establishing a comprehensive lead in cost reduction over its rivals. In other words, it is the most cost-efficient producer in its segment. Its cost leadership relates to average total costs and creates potential for the company to cut prices. Its fundamental aim is to reduce costs below those of its competitors, but without falling below the level of service and quality its customers expect.

Make a distinction between cost and price leadership

This point must be emphasized: Cost leadership does not just mean being cheaper than the competition. In essence, cost leadership means having a relative advantage in total costs that is generally also reflected in low prices. However, the level of quality and service expected in the particular market segment in question must also be maintained. Nor should the price effect be given undue prominence. Cost advantages impact initially on a company's profitability, which generates resources for additional investment, for example, in research, improved production processes, or expanding the company (increasing market share through acquisitions). Such investment can lead, in turn, to increases in overall productivity.

In order successfully to pursue a cost-leadership strategy, a broadly based market must exist in which a number of different segments are serviced. In certain circumstances, the players may also be active in related sectors. The large retail groups are good examples of such market configurations. In Germany, for instance, the former cash-and-carry specialist Metro now also operates outlets such as Real (supermarkets), Media/Saturn (electrical goods), Kaufhof (department stores), and Praktiker (home-improvement stores). Thus, the cost advantage can work in two directions. It can impact on the market, with the cost leader increasing its market share as a result of its lower prices (while maintaining quality and service levels to the greatest possible extent). Conversely, it can impact on the company itself, with the improved cost structure leading to higher profitability. The company's economic efficiency and financial power guarantee it a superior competitive position.

Commit yourself to a price strategy

There are two types of price strategies: the no-frills strategy and the low-price supplier. A no-frills strategy combines low price with low additional utility. Companies that adopt this approach are offering customers a basic product that fulfills an existing basic need, but not a jot more: no image, no design, no ambience, and no service. Consider discounters such as Aldi or airlines like easyJet. The basic principle of both companies is quite simple. Aldi says, "Our customers want cheap basic foodstuffs. This is what we give them. No frippery – flour is flour and milk is milk." And easyJet? Price is everything. When the average passenger jets off on vacation, the on-board service just doesn't matter. And for companies as well. A 50 percent cost reduction is more important than supplying middle managers with tasteless sandwiches on flights lasting only an hour.

A company adopting a low-price strategy is trying to reduce its prices while maintaining comparable quality and service levels (with regard to decor and fittings, quality, and differentiation, for example). This is dangerous for a company that prices aggressively when there is no obvious cost advantage. One common consequence of this strategy is that competitors enter the price war and reduce profit margins for all the players. The winner will be the cost leader in the industry. This is why any company pursuing a low-price strategy should always make sure that its cost structures give it a competitive advantage.

Identify the potential for cost leadership

Whenever cost leadership is discussed, terms such as the learning (or experience) curve, economies of scale, economies of scope, and economies of learning tend to be bandied about. What does all this mean? In the mid 1960s, the Boston Consulting Group described the connection between a product's cost evolution and the cumulative output. The key message of the study was that if the cumulative output of a product doubles over the course of the entire production period, then unit costs (adjusted for inflation) fall by as much as 20–30 percent. Economies of scale are achieved by increasing output, and economies of scope reduce costs because resources are used more efficiently for several product categories.

What is the reason for this effect? Analysis of the learning curve makes it possible to identify economies of scale and learning that are achieved over time. All other things being equal, economies of scale mean that unit costs fall as plant size increases. The basic notion underlying the principle of economies of learning is that workers' experience produces learning effects that lead to improved production processes and/or optimized structures. The third strategic approach to cost reduction is based on the notion of economies of scope. The term denotes production-cost advantages generated by combining the production of different products. Such advantages are achieved when a company is able to produce a number of different products together more cheaply than an independent producer making each product separately. The reason for these cost savings lies in the shared use of capacities and resources.

Two examples can usefully be cited here. Under the aegis of Ferdinand Piëch, the VW group put into practice a platform-sharing strategy, in which four different platforms were used to produce more than 20 different vehicles for four core brands (VW, Audi, Skoda, and Seat). At the same time, a part-sharing approach was put into practice as early as the design phase; this too gave rise to economies of scope. Platform A is the basis for the Golf, the new Beetle, the Audi A3 and TT, the Seat Toledo, and the Skoda Octavia. From the cost point of view, this is undoubtedly an optimal principle. However, if image factors such as brand and vehicle profile are taken into account, then there must be a fear that a cannibalization effect could set in, particularly among the higher-value brands. Why pay for an Audi when a Skoda is made from the same components?

News organizations that supply program material for various media platforms provide another example of economies of scope. Thus, in Germany, N24 is the news provider for a total of four television channels, which would otherwise all have their own news departments. And in Britain, ITN provides news for ITV, Channel 4, and Five, as well as for commercial radio stations. The broadcaster's job, ultimately, is just to stamp the channel's own branding on the news provided by an external supplier. In the context of the learning curve, the strategic consequence for cost leaders is obvious: They must try to increase their output in order to increase their competitive advantage over their rivals. The supplier who, at a given point in time, has the largest cumulative output will in all probability have the largest market share and the lowest unit costs. Hence, competition based on costs is also competition based on output volumes.

Consider a few success factors in developing cost-leadership strategies

What strategic success factors must companies consider if they are going to put the cost-leadership strategy into practice? If one asks these days for examples of cost leadership in Germany, there is a 99 percent probability that Aldi will be the first name to be mentioned. Everybody automatically associates the retail giant with consistently high quality and constantly low prices. Aldi has committed itself to the discount principle: concentration on the essentials. In successfully implementing the cost-leadership strategy, the company has made every effort to put into practice a strategy geared to large-scale purchasing ("effective purchasing management"). The purchasing department buys in goods as cheaply as possible. In doing so, there are various ways of converting even secondary effects into purchasing advantages.

- Aldi awards long-term, high-volume contracts that allow producers to operate their plant and equipment more consistently and in a more focused way. This makes it easier for them to make decisions on technical progress and production modernization, which in turn enables them to produce at lower cost.
- As a result of Aldi's long-term purchasing guarantee, producers are able largely to dispense with advertising for their products. Consequently, their goods are more or less unencumbered by advertising costs.
- However, even less significant arrangements produce additional purchasing advantages, such as the promise that deliveries can be made in full trucks or the abandonment of superfluous packaging.

These examples show very clearly that, at Aldi, the foundation for low sales prices is laid in the purchasing department. Sales prices are also influenced by the business situation. The rents paid for Aldi's stores represent a significant proportion of the sales price. The company makes every effort to keep this factor as low as possible as well. Its efforts in this respect find visible expression in the practical, utilitarian design of Aldi stores. Ostentatious architecture is most definitely not on the agenda. Moreover, they are often not sited in the usual business locations, but increasingly on the edge of inner cities or on the outskirts of towns, where rents are lower than in established shopping areas. These locations also have extensive parking lots, which make it easier for consumers to do their shopping. It is worth driving the extra distance, since lower rents also contribute to lower sales prices.

Every day, enormous quantities of goods are transported in order to ensure that Aldi stores receive their deliveries reliably and on time. This massive logistical operation takes place with all the precision of a Swiss watch. Workers ready for action, perfect organization, many years' experience, and state-of-the-art transportation equipment all help to make the entire exercise as efficient and cost-effective as possible, which ultimately is reflected in low prices. A visit to an Aldi store will reveal the secret of these low prices: Sugar, flour, drinks, milk, detergents, and other products are often piled high on pallets that have been packed by machines at the manufacturers, so that Aldi workers do not actually have to handle the goods at all. All other items are piled together on pallets in the storeroom and then taken by forklift truck to the sales floor. Once there, it is usually sufficient just to set down the container, the contents of which will have already been made ready for sale, and cut it open or remove the perforated side. Nobody at Aldi is concerned in the slightest with the aesthetics of product display.

The Aldi principle is to stock as few of the same or similar types of product as possible. This principle gives rise to cost advantages and is reflected in low prices. By severely restricting its product range, the company can sell every single item in large quantities and at low prices. In this way, the labor required – from the receipt of goods in the central warehouse to the storing position on the sales floor – can be deployed under optimal conditions. Goods are turned over very quickly, which in turn means low interest charges. These advantages facilitate cost accounting and lead to low sales prices. The company management attaches great importance to the fact that Aldi will not spend a single Euro more than is absolutely necessary. As a result of this philosophy, large sums are saved whenever Aldi opens a new store or renovates an existing one, which again impacts favorably on pricing.

Successful cost leaders have different strategies. Nevertheless, a number of success factors can be highlighted.

Cost leaders in their own segment. It is not enough to be second best. Not until your total costs are permanently lower than the competition can you actually implement the cost-leadership strategy. This in turn implies that cost leaders have constantly to strive to optimize their costs. Costs and processes are the focus of management action.

Effective purchasing management. The ruling principle in purchasing and development is "design to cost" (in the sense of "design to save money"), in which product and service design must adhere to maximum cost targets. These targets are geared to the costs of competitors in the same market segment. Nevertheless, it is customer requirements that set the basic parameters for quality, design, level of service, and fittings. They must be met. In the design-to-cost philosophy, however, the deciding factor is not the construction of the product price, but rather the interplay between cost targets and market requirements. Additional factors that help to optimize purchasing management include the use of standardized materials, parts, and components and close collaboration with selected suppliers, with whom strategic partnerships are established in order jointly to pursue quality and cost targets. Another decisive factor, of course, is the calculation of cost-optimal order volumes. Cost leaders must take advantage of economies of scale in purchasing (a gradual decrease in unit costs as a result of larger order volumes, increased bargaining power, and optimized order processing), and adopt intelligent purchasing and warehousing strategies in order to minimize costs. A further requirement is an optimized sourcing strategy that seeks to take advantage of globalization: Cost leaders scour the world for the cheapest supplies of their staple items. The example of that famous southern German specialty the pretzel illustrates how far the globalization of purchasing has now gone. Pretzels, hard salted biscuits, usually in the form of a knot, are one of the cultural treasures of Bavaria and Swabia most worthy of preservation; nowadays, they are supplied to cost-conscious bakers preshaped but raw and frozen. After the collapse of the Iron Curtain, the cheapest raw pretzels came from Eastern Europe, initially the Czech Republic, later Poland. Where do the cheapest ones come from today? The labels on the pretzels destined for Bavaria now declare "Made in Hong Kong." Don't choke on your pretzel!

Highest overall productivity in the industry. Cost leaders have production in mind even at the design stage. It is important, therefore, to practice simultaneous product and process development (simultaneous engineering). They concentrate on their core competences and outsource all activities that can be carried out more cheaply by suppliers. Furthermore, outsourcing enables cost leaders to buy in a high degree of flexibility and to minimize risk. If demand falls, suppliers can usually be given notice more easily than direct employees. And if demand rises, a company can call on new suppliers who are too expensive when demand is low. In cost-leader companies, the make-or-buy policy is optimized. Furthermore, gradual reductions in costs can be achieved through high unit volumes and intelligent production processes. Cost leaders avoid low batch sizes and special orders or custom-made products. Production processes are geared to producing the maximum output rate for each unit of capacity per unit of time, ensuring the highest possible capacity and resource utilization, and avoiding any defective products and subsequent rectification measures. Management approaches that support these objectives include TQM systems (zero-fault strategy) and the lean management principle, which revolutionized the car industry at the beginning of the 1990s and then spread to other areas of the manufacturing sector.

Concentration of capital utilized. All fixed and working assets that are not required for the company's core competences are eliminated. Investment in production plant, buildings, and other facilities is concentrated on what is essential, the overriding objective being always to increase productivity. Receivables and stock are reduced to the lowest possible levels.

The cost leader's corporate culture. Cost leadership demands an uncompromising approach to cost reduction and a commitment to seek out potential for cost optimization at all levels. Ingvar Kamprad – founder of IKEA, furnisher of countless student hovels, and cause of even more nervous breakdowns (where's the screw?) – has made scrimping his ruling principle, in both his personal and his business life. Executives have to fly economy class, stay in cheap hotels, and basically eat in the staff cafeteria. Kamprad himself prefers to take the bus rather than an expensive taxi, unless of course he is on the road in his ancient Volvo. According to IKEA mythology, he uses disposable plates twice and likes

to invite business colleagues to eat at the company's own hot-dog stall
– and does so frequently. It is taken for granted that IKEA should optimize costs at all levels of its operations. Production is completely
outsourced to suppliers right across the world, from Hungary to
Vietnam, and the company's legal structure is used to minimize its tax
burden. However, what emerges most clearly from a description of the
company's quirky founder is that cost leadership begins with a mental
attitude. Executives and top managers must lead the way by making
cost awareness a way of life that is implemented rigorously throughout
the company. Strict financial control and the reduction of overhead
costs to the absolute minimum are all part of the cost leader's armory.
A culture of this kind can be developed only over the long term. This
is why it is difficult for a differentiator to change quickly to a cost-
leadership strategy or even to implement a hybrid strategy.

Organizational measures. A cost leader usually has a sophisticated
reporting and controlling system, which is followed through with the
utmost consistency. For this reason, expenditure on control and
coordination in cost-oriented companies is generally very high.
Furthermore, the organizational structure is clearly defined and
strictly managed. In the production department in particular, there is a
complex division of labor and a high degree of specialization. And
there are incentive systems geared to quantitative targets, such as
meeting cost targets.

Adopt a systematic approach to the identification of potential cost reductions

The value chain is a key strategic instrument for identifying and real-
izing competitive advantages. It is the starting point for strategic cost
analysis, which in turn forms the basis of a cost-leadership strategy. A
company breaks the value chain down into the strategically relevant
activities that are necessary for the production process, and hence for
the creation of a product or service. These activities can be divided into
primary and supporting activities. Primary activities are those directly
linked to the creation and distribution of the product (inbound and
outbound logistics, production, sales, customer service). They are the

value-creating activities. Purchasing, human resource management, R&D, and the company infrastructure are supporting activities.

Cost leaders are in control of their value-creation process and are able to shape this process creatively in order to achieve significant cost reductions. This is one of the important factors in achieving competitive advantages by adopting a cost-leadership strategy. The company must succeed in breaking away from its industry's characteristic organizing principle, as many Japanese companies did in the 1980s with the introduction of kaizen, the kanban system, and just-in-time production. The fundamental objective is to manufacture products differently from the competition and to deviate from the well-trodden path. Examine your processes and look for measures you can take that will produce considerable cost reductions. We will look later in detail at an innovative approach to fundamental and radical cost optimization known as business reengineering.

In order to achieve a competitive advantage, individual activities must be carried out more cheaply or more profitably than in competitor firms. Take the example of the German company Würth. As a world leader in the supply of assembly materials, the company has achieved a high degree of cost optimization and customer loyalty through the vertical interlocking of its processes with those of its customers. The company's products are in themselves rather insignificant: Screws, bolts, washers, and so on, which are produced in large volumes but are of little value individually, actually leave little scope for entrepreneurial imagination and innovation. Würth, however, begs to differ – Würth thinks systemically and in terms of processes. What problems do customers have in handling our products? How can we optimize the processes associated with ordering and storing our products? Würth has put its customers' processes under the microscope and has come to the following conclusion: What our customers are reluctant to do, we can do for them. So Würth monitors customers' stock, triggers orders, and arranges for products to be stored. Every distributor's dream.

The ideas for putting this concept into practice are as simple as they are ingenious. For example, the company has installed networked scales under the screw containers. These replace regular stock controls by warehouse staff. If the weight of the screw containers falls below a certain threshold level, an order is sent to Würth via the data link connecting the customer's scales to the manufacturer's computer system. In this way, the entire ordering process (internally and then to the supplier) is rendered superfluous by having a purchasing department located on the customer's premises. Würth delivers to 97 percent of customers within 24 hours. When the goods are delivered to the customer, the invoice is issued via the Würth system, the new stock level is entered at the customer's end, and the accounts are audited. The advantages for the customer are obvious: perfect stock control and an optimized ordering system at minimal cost. Cost awareness and utility maximization are here combined. And Würth itself gains by obtaining maximum customer loyalty, since the barriers to exit are extremely high for customers. With this level of service, who is going to move to another supplier? Thus, Würth is a differentiator, since the company can obviously allow itself to be more expensive than the competition. At the same time, however, Würth does reduce costs for its customers, since logistical and ordering processes can be outsourced.

For this reason, strategic cost analysis lies at the heart of the cost-leadership strategy. It is an ideal method of generating cost advantages and optimizing processes. Of course, companies that are essentially not seeking to adopt a cost-leadership strategy can also benefit from the method, since it is in every company's interest to optimize its cost situation. The difference between cost leaders and differentiating competitors, however, lies in the fact that, for a cost leader, the main focus of attention must be management of the cost position. Implement the following five measures in order to establish your competitive position as a cost leader.

1. *Describe your value chain.* What primary activities make up your value-creation process? Examine the individual value-creation processes closely. It is helpful in doing so to divide up the separate stages in greater detail than in the basic model.

2. *Calculate the costs for each individual stage of the value chain.* This sounds simple, but in practice is very laborious and complex. Cost allocation is carried out along the same lines as cost-center accounting. Direct costs are attributed to the relevant activities. Overheads are attributed to the activities generating the costs on a pro rata basis. Since you are engaging here in a strategic cost analysis, all cost factors should be treated as subject to influence. Produce a

graphical representation of your analysis, with the larger cost pools in the value chain also depicted larger on the graph or chart.

3. *Identify the cost drivers.* Cost drivers are cost-determining factors that are dependent on variable commercial factors. These include, for example, establishment size, location, experience and learning effects, the structure of capacity utilization, and the linkage between the various elements of the value chain. In purchasing, for example, the following cost drivers can be identified: order size, the number of suppliers (the more suppliers there are, the higher the coordination costs), and bargaining power (on both the suppliers' and customers' side). Well-known customers frequently enjoy cost advantages over less prestigious purchasers. Examine the product-development department. What are the cost drivers here? The more diverse the development commissions are, the higher the costs. By encouraging interplant or interdepartmental cooperation, one development process could be carried out for a number of different products, for example. In the assembly department, cost drivers include plant size and percentage utilization, employee experience, and the degree of automation. Concentrate on the cost pools that appear largest on the chart. There is no point wasting time on a process that accounts for only 0.5 percent of total costs, if there is scope for savings in the larger cost pools.

4. *Identify connections and interactions.* In this fourth stage, ask yourself the following question: To what extent do decisions and actions taken at one stage in the value-creation process determine costs at another? Let us cite a few examples. Product design (development) affects not only the production processes but also warehousing and distribution. Or again, the more comprehensive the quality controls are (cost-raising factor), the fewer claims or complaints there will be (cost-reduction factor). You also need to analyze those factors influencing costs that, say, can be attributed to suppliers. Integrating your own value chain with upstream and downstream chains is a basic necessity, of course. Thus, incoming goods inspection, for instance, can be outsourced to the supplier, as is usual in the car industry. The relevant contracts stipulate that deliveries to the major manufacturers should be fault-free. Consequently, suppliers are forced to satisfy their customers'

requirements in every particular if they do not want to be crossed off the list of approved suppliers.

5. *Compile a list of actions.* Go ahead and draw up an action plan for reducing costs. In practice, the implementation of cost-optimization programs is one of the most problematic steps, since restructurings and cost savings are inextricably associated with anxieties about one's own survival or loss of power. On the employees' side, some of the concepts associated with reengineering and lean management should have released positive energies and a willingness to implement the measures required. Here, a combination of employee involvement and rigorous leadership phases is appropriate (Box 8.1).

1. *Involvement.* Change thinking and culture in the company: "Cost reduction is positive and safeguards jobs."
2. *Leadership.* Set cost-reduction targets. These targets should be binding and apply to all functions within the company. It is not only the purchasing or production departments that are responsible for cost management, but the marketing department and the administration as well.
3. *Involvement.* Encourage employees to help identify potential for cost reductions. Set cost-reduction targets, and ask departments and individual employees to suggest ways in which costs can be reduced. Additionally, it is worth while setting up cross-functional project teams and giving them the task of analyzing the links and interactions between the individual stages of the value chain.
4. *Leadership.* Demand that the measures be implemented rigorously. Binding project steps, a clear schedule, and an effective controlling system must exist so that the cost-optimization process can proceed successfully.
5. *Involvement.* Communicate intensively: Employees must be continuously informed of analyses, actions, and results.

Box 8.1: Implementation of cost-optimization programs

Shape the corporate processes: Business-process reengineering

The purpose of reengineering is to analyze a company's key processes and restructure them in a more efficient way, without regard for the boundaries between functions that have prevailed hitherto. Business reengineering means abandoning certain existing approaches and procedures, and considering the work process from a new perspective in order to offer the customer enhanced value. In practical terms, it means answering the following question: If you had to set up this company again with the knowledge you now have and the current state of technology, what would it look like? Breaking down the functional units into their individual processes and putting them back together again in a less vertical form will reveal where the company has run to fat and can be slimmed down.

The notion of reengineering was developed at the beginning of the 1990s by Michael Hammer and James Champy (1996), head of the management consultancy CSC. It evolved in the same way as many popular management theories: from research conducted by an academic, via its marketing by a management consultancy and a best-selling book, to its short-lived status as a panacea for all corporate ills. However, reengineering was of as little use for that purpose as any other management formula. Its popularity was due in part to the authors' ability to produce memorable sound bites; this applied particularly to Hammer's statements. Nevertheless, the approach was implemented by a number of well-known companies with considerable success. The greeting-card maker Hallmark, for example, reengineered its entire innovation process, while Kodak succeeded in halving its reaction time to new orders by applying this procedure to the production process for black-and-white films.

The optimization or reengineering of critical business processes is the actual core of innovation and excellence in production. The most important strategies and behavioral rules for successful process reengineering are listed below.

● Concentration is on the most important horizontal processes in production: the selection, training, and motivation of direct and indirect personnel and management; the selection, development, and management of suppliers; the simultaneous development and improvement of products and production processes; the specification, acquisition, installation, and maintenance of plant and machinery; effective management of the entire supply chain.

- An approach is adopted that is simultaneously top-down (targets) and bottom-up (solutions), with the active involvement of all those involved in multidisciplinary teams; employees take decisions; several posts are merged into one (a generalist or team takes over the entire process).
- The individual process steps are arranged into a natural sequence (artificial linear sequences are abolished); each process has several variants (the end of standardization – a breakdown into simple, moderately difficult, and difficult processes); work is done where it makes most sense to do it; the need for supervision and control is reduced.
- Coordination effort is reduced to a minimum.
- The case manager is the sole contact point for the customer.
- Efforts must be made simultaneously to address problems with throughput times, costs, and quality.
- Actions always proceed from the outside in, beginning with the customer (whether external or internal).
- The factory gates do not have a stop sign; customers and suppliers should be involved.
- Effective, that is, frequent and often repeated, communication is important; this is something many managers underestimate.

Like all modern business theories, business reengineering seeks to release natural abilities and emphasizes human creativity. Its underlying principle, therefore, is not the imposition of a single model for all, but the opposite: namely, the development of specific individual skills. However, these skills are strictly subordinated to the demands of the market. All business processes are called into question in a radical way. Those processes that do not produce value added are reduced, not simply improved. The organization of the remaining tasks is no longer based on a functional division of labor, but is process-oriented. The processes themselves are defined in terms of direct customer utility, not of posts and job tasks.

The approach is a very basic one. The first question to be asked is why such and such a task is performed. Only then do we inquire as to how it might be done. No superficial changes are made; rather, the company is completely reshaped. This leads to considerable improvements (not just by a few percentage points, but many times over!). It is also important to focus on the customer's order, with generalists taking responsibility for implementing the process in a holistic way, rather than having individual steps completed by specialists. Business reengineering should not start with individual parts of an organization, since it is precisely such structural divisions that are being called into question.

For employees, work content changes fundamentally. They are no longer required to complete a set of tasks prescribed by their supervisor, but instead to take personal responsibility for fulfilling the customer's requirements. The market now presses individual workers hard. As a result, they need to market their own performance. In some ways, this can be regarded as job enrichment; on the other hand, however, it also increases the pressure on workers, not so much in the sense of an abstract pressure to perform, but rather of a compulsion increasingly to extend their own skills.

How is a differentiation strategy developed?

Why do customers prefer an Audi over a Skoda, despite the fact that the cars are largely identical? Why do people take a British Airways flight for £400 when they could fly with easyJet or Ryanair for £99? What attracts people to expensive restaurants when they can eat their fill more cheaply in a fast-food joint? Differentiation means offering customers products or services that provide them with additional utility, by means of which a company can set itself apart from the competition on a lasting basis. Thus, a differentiation strategy focuses on performance rather than costs. Customers opt to buy products or services not on the basis of prices, but because they provide value added for which they are prepared to pay a premium price. Hence, a differentiation strategy requires two things.

Customer acceptance. The value added must be perceptible to customers. In practice, it is frequently the case that performance characteristics are not perceived at all by customers, or not regarded as valuable. The supplier, on the other hand, is of the opinion that the factors providing the value added represent particular performance characteristics.

Differentiation from the competition. Here, too, it is necessary to ascertain by analyzing the competition which performance characteristics have a differentiating effect that sets the products or services in question apart from the competition. There can be no talk of a differentiation advantage unless certain performance characteristics are better than those of the competition and cannot be easily imitated, thereby conferring a lasting competitive advantage. Anything else is just floating around in the no man's land of mediocrity.

Accordingly, the differentiating characteristics have a great deal in common with the attributes that confer enduring competitive advantages, although they are located at the level of products and services rather than the company's capabilities and resources. Differentiating characteristics must also be valuable to customers, not widely available in the market, difficult for competitors to imitate, and not readily substitutable. If a company also succeeds in placing the differentiating characteristics on a sound and lasting footing in the market, then it is possible to speak of a genuine competitive advantage. Permanence demands that the costs of differentiation must be covered over the entire period by a correspondingly high level of earnings. Furthermore, a differentiating company's rate of return must be higher than that of its competitors precisely because of the differentiation. If competitors imitate the differentiating characteristics, the pioneer must already have generated sufficient earnings to allow the company to obtain competitive advantages at different levels and by means of different characteristics.

Like cost leaders, differentiators do not have a strong competitive advantage over their rivals unless they are the only differentiator in the market. In this respect, it helps to have very tightly defined market segments. Differentiators must have a clearly defined target group in mind. To that extent, differentiation tends towards smaller market segments than cost leadership. Differentiation relies on quality, particular specifications, or a well-thought-out service formula. These characteristics are generally geared to the concrete requirements of a narrowly defined group of customers. Consider BMW, for example.

Even if the manufacturer is active in the mass car market, every car meets the requirements of small market segments. The sporty z4 is targeted at well-off two-car owners who want a smart, impressive car to help with their weekend shopping. The BMW 7 series, which is equipped with Internet access, satisfies the needs of successful business people who want to be permanently available and online.

For this reason, differentiation tends towards tighter focusing. At a time when people define themselves in terms of their individuality, mass markets are becoming highly segmented. The flour sold at Aldi does not have to satisfy any desire for individuality; it just has to be cheap. This is one requirement of an undifferentiated mass market. However, high-value products give expression to people's individuality and their attitudes to life.

Identify your differentiation drivers

What are the differentiating characteristics in which a company can place its hopes, whether it is in the service or manufacturing sector, or whether it is selling to end users or to industrial customers?

Differentiating factor 1: Equipment and facilities. A company can set itself apart from the competition by means of a leading-edge technology or the particular scope of its services. Differentiation driven by innovation was considered in detail in the section on the various phases of competition, since the main objective here is to convert a chronological lead into economic success. Differentiation also sets in with the question: "What range of services does the end user receive for a particular end price?" The more comprehensive the service package, the more highly esteemed the products and services on offer. Today, a navigation system is an accessory that is installed only in certain vehicles, for which customers pay a premium price. ABS braking systems, on the other hand, are a standard fitting in all classes of vehicle. Thus, differentiating factors frequently start off being exclusive or even unique, and then become standard features without any special value rating.

Differentiating factor 2: Quality. Why are customers prepared to pay more for quality products than for the competition's cheaper offerings?

We have known the reason since we were children: Good products last longer because there are fewer faults. The quality is better. Better materials were used to produce them, the workers were highly skilled, and thus the workmanship is better. The result is a quality product, such as knife blades from Solingen, top wines from Piedmont, or precision instruments and machinery from the Swabian Alps. Customers pay more for such products because utilization costs over the product's lifetime are lower.

Differentiating factor 3: Service. In today's competitive environment, firms have to be quicker (12-hour delivery service), more flexible (available 365 days a year), and more friendly than the competition. Service-oriented companies offer their customers unique services, which sometimes even the customers themselves are not expecting, such as extensive advice on what to purchase, free assembly of equipment, integrated monitoring systems, free maintenance, assumption of responsibility for disposal, advice on processes, involvement of the customer in product development, and the provision of customer-specific solutions. These are only a few examples that lead to differentiation through service. For many years, Putzmeister, a world leader in concrete pumps, has analyzed when spare parts are required in which machines. In order to spare their customers unnecessary downtime, the company supplies the critical parts at the right time. This is a service that benefits both parties. The customer gains a high degree of protection against downtime, while Putzmeister enjoys a high level of turnover from its service activities and raises its customer-satisfaction ratings into the bargain.

Thus, analysis of customers' value chain is an important preliminary step in organizing services in a demand-oriented way. The company must get to grips with its customers' value-creation process and analyze the extent to which it can create value added through the services it provides. This means that the company's processes are closely coordinated with those of its customers. As you implement the differentiation strategy, you will discover that all the other differentiating factors also impact on the customers' value chain, and thus have to be taken into account in the analysis.

The element of surprise is of decisive importance with services, in which personal experience of the product plays such a crucial role. Customers display little awareness of standard services. However, exceptional services that fly in the face of industry standards permanently set a company apart. The supervised play area in IKEA stores, which otherwise provide no services for customers at all, gives many families with children an opportunity to relax while doing their shopping. This service is unknown in other large stores and creates an image of a family-friendly furniture paradise for IKEA. This too makes it clear that service standards are defined by reference to the industry as a whole.

Differentiating factor 4: Design. Bang and Olufsen are a prime example of differentiation through exceptional design. The unique visual appearance of the company's hi-fi systems gives them a real allure and clearly sets them apart from the competition. Or ask Braun's customers: It is not only the product quality that is persuasive, but also the design legend that has been created over the past 50 years. Design does not have to coincide with mass taste, but must offer customers value added through its unique selling point and individuality. Drivers of an old Saab or a Volvo shaped like a breadbox are aware that they are sitting not in the most beautiful, but at least in an exceptional, vehicle – a car that stands out from the mass of cars by virtue of its shape. For aesthetes, design is certainly a quality criterion. However, extraordinary design can compensate even for the mediocrity of the rest of the offer. To that extent, the influence of design as a competitive factor should be regarded as a separate differentiating criterion.

Differentiating factor 5: Image. At a time when products are becoming increasingly interchangeable, a product's signaling effect is an important factor in its competitive success. Consider the market for branded cigarettes. These are products that all taste more or less the same, have no particular performance characteristics, and cost pretty much the same as each other. Consequently, the only way of ensuring a brand's survival amid the welter of virtually indistinguishable competing products is to build up an image, to create a world associated with the brand. Thus, Stuyvesant smokers are multicultural, users of Ecover detergent are concerned about the environment, and viewers of the Arte television channel are intellectuals. Products create identification, both for outsiders and for consumers themselves.

Consider a few success factors in developing differentiation strategies

A guest arrives at the Hotel Adlon in Berlin. The car door is opened smartly, and from that first moment onward the guest is treated with extraordinary warmth and courtesy. Since paying the taxi driver is time-consuming and possibly even strenuous, the friendly doorman suggests that the hotel might pay the fare and charge it to the guest's account. No time is wasted in getting into the warmth of the hotel. It goes without saying that guests have nothing to do with carrying their luggage. Once inside the hotel, guests are addressed by name right from the start and treated at all times with great professionalism. Regular guests even have their favorite brand of cigarettes waiting for them in their rooms. Those rooms are fitted out to the highest possible standard. There are several restaurants to choose from, as well as an exclusive fitness center and several business lounges for guests to use (provided they have the ability to be in two places at once). The clientele is well-to-do and may even include a few celebrities. All these factors conspire to increase guests' awareness that they are staying in a place of unrivaled exclusivity. Another nice touch is that guests' shoes are cleaned overnight. Even if they're left outside the room at three o'clock in the morning, there they'll be three hours later, freshly polished, glaring up at the sleepy occupant. People are very willing to pay a premium price for such a high level of service and quality. And what is more, the Hotel Adlon has clearly set itself apart from the competition. Successful differentiation strategies, such as those adopted by the Adlon, have certain characteristics in common.

They create customer value. Differentiation must represent value for the customer. This may be because the customer's costs are reduced or because efficiency is improved.

They impact positively on the company's own value chain. It is necessary, first, to analyze the value chain of one's own company, with each stage of the value-creation process being investigated in order to ascertain how much it contributes to differentiation of the company's offer. A service-oriented company must ask the following question at each stage of the value-creation process: To what extent does such-and-such an activity help to improve our service quality? In the case of a bank examining the sales stage of its value chain, for example, this means asking: What measures need to be taken in order to optimize the advice our employees give to customers? Or what information can be given to customers so that they feel they have been given the best possible advice in purchasing the products they require?

They impact positively on the customer's value chain. Knowledge and networking within the customer's value chain can also produce value added, which is another important element of a differentiation strategy. For this reason, companies adopting such a strategy must possess considerable knowledge in their customers' value-creation processes. They must try to influence their customers' value-driving activities by means of the products or services they themselves provide. One way of achieving this is for suppliers to network their processes with those of customers. Networking of this kind will not only enhance value in the short term, but also create close links between customers and suppliers.

They create customer value through premium prices. At the end of the 1990s, New York was experiencing the frenzy of the dot-com boom. Service was high on the agenda at that time. Kozmo and Urbanfetch, who have now disappeared from the market, had rediscovered delivery services. From videos to Häagen-Dazs ice cream, from the latest Palm Pilot to the current bestseller – Kozmo and Urbanfetch sent out demoniacal cyclists to deliver whatever the stressed acolytes of the new economy desired. Not at a time convenient for the supplier, but quickly, with an agreed response time 24/7 irrespective of the item to be delivered. Moreover, this value added was offered at no cost. There was no extra charge for the delivery service; the goods were simply delivered at the low prices customary in the particular market in question. Orders were taken over the Internet, with customers being offered maximum convenience. The result was obvious: Customers enthusiastically ordered goods at normal retail prices, and each delivery was subsidized by risk capital made available by the venture-capital firms. The customers never understood the true value of the service, and so the concept was doomed to failure. As far as the differentiation strategy is concerned, this example demonstrates two things. First, value added must self-evidently be converted into a market price. Second, this price must correspond to the value perceived by the customer. In this respect, value signals are of crucial importance in the differentiation strategy. Ask yourself how you make clear the value of your products or services. In giving its customers a purchase certificate signed by its management board, the luxury carmaker Maybach is making clear that purchasers of its vehicles are part of an exclusive clientele. Even the obstacles that have to be overcome to gain entry to a famous business school are important factors in documenting the value of the course of study: The more difficult it is to get a place, the better the business school appears to be.

They are based on knowledge of the real customer. Who is actually buying your products? The real customers are not anonymous companies, but individual decision-makers. Their needs and purchasing criteria have to be met. If you deal with large organizations, it is often buying centers that are responsible for purchasing decisions; in the case of families, it is often the family board that decides. To that extent, it is important to examine in detail not only the decision-makers, but also the entire decision-making process. Who makes the decision? How do decision-making processes proceed? What are the relevant purchasing criteria? Who decides on which purchasing criteria? How does a customer define customer value?

They take the customer's real purchasing criteria into account. The customer's purchasing criteria must be considered individually and analyzed closely. Why does a customer opt for a particular product? Such decisions are not necessarily taken on rational grounds. Image and cautious thinking, as well as various irrational and emotional reasons, are all factors that influence purchasing decisions. Thus, more than 90 percent of the criteria in insurance purchasing decisions are influenced by irrational factors. There are basically two types of motivating factors. Use criteria are product characteristics that reduce costs or enhance performance. These may be functionality, quality, delivery times, and service. Signal criteria are characteristics from which the customer can draw conclusions about the product's value. These may be factors related to image, such as advertising, design, or even employee behavior. Against this background, marketing and design play an important role for differentiators. Just look at the fashion or perfume industries, where differentiation is pursued by means of enormous marketing budgets. Customers are unable to tell the products apart in advertisements (scratch-and-sniff cards or perfume sachets being exceptions) but only through targeted image-building, which positions the products within the target group's lifestyle.

They see differentiation as a set of differentiating criteria. Even though individual differentiating criteria may be crucial to certain companies, differentiation strategies generally have to rely on several criteria. Using a single differentiating characteristic to position a company becomes risky, ultimately, when competitors are able to imitate that characteristic. Only a few companies succeed in setting themselves apart from the competition on the basis of a single differentiating characteristic. On the other hand, consider a differentiating brand such as Mercedes-Benz, in which technology, service, manufacturing quality, and image all combine to confer uniqueness on the company's products. Bang and Olufsen differentiate themselves not only through their unique design, but also through their exclusive sales outlets and exceptional expenditure on communication.

They understand that differentiation means setting oneself apart. Differentiation is kept alive not only by exceptional customer competence, but also by excellent understanding of the competition. As a differentiator, you must know precisely what value added your competitors offer, where in their value chain the value-driving activities are located, and the extent to which your output actually differs from the competition. Companies frequently make the mistake of regarding standards as differentiating criteria. Anybody today considering buying a BMW 7 series or a Mercedes S class is provided with excellent information material and splendid brochures. However, these marketing instruments are not differentiating characteristics. Their substitutability makes them an industry standard. What has to be done, by adopting appropriate methods, is to identify which performance characteristics constitute standards, what customers perceive as valuable, and the means whereby value added is created for which customers are actually prepared to pay. Ask yourself the question: What actually distinguishes us from our competitors and what do our customers obtain only from us?

They subscribe to a value-driven corporate culture. In our analysis of cost leadership, it became clear that mental attitude matters. The same applies to a differentiation strategy. Anyone seeking to generate value added must adopt a value-driven approach. This requires space for creativity, generosity (within the bounds of cost-effectiveness), individuality, and a risk-taking innovation culture. At the same time, many companies that have adopted a differentiation strategy clearly have a love of their product and a high degree of customer orientation. Here, too, it would take decades to convert a value-driven corporate culture into a cost-conscious culture. This is why it is important to decide definitively on a company's positioning.

Adopt a systematic approach to the identification of differentiation potential

Whether you are dealing with an industrial company investing in capital goods, such as a new forklift truck, or a family contemplating the purchase of consumer services, such as its annual vacation, the following eight actions can be reviewed in order to put in place a well-thought-out differentiation strategy. The examples listed are intended to point up what lies behind the individual steps in the system. It should be noted at this point that the authors have considerable experience in the purchase and sale of travel services, but are able to draw only on good amateur knowledge when it comes to developing a differentiation strategy for forklift-truck manufacturers. Thus, the following examples should be regarded merely as pointers for those seeking a better understanding of the method, and not as instructions for setting up a forklift-truck company.

1. *Establish who the real purchaser is.* The first step should be to realize that the identification of the real purchaser is of decisive importance. Such a realization encourages you to focus not on institutional customers, on an anonymous entity with no decision-making powers, but rather on the individual with the authority to make purchasing decisions. This is why it is essential to be absolutely clear about who in your client company (which may also include distribution partners and dealers) generally makes purchasing decisions: Is it individual buyers, buying centers, cross-functional purchasing committees, or, in the case of prestige decisions, the most senior executives? You must also find out whether there are any upper limits on purchases, so that you can contact the right buyers.

However, anyone seeking to generate customer-driven value added on a lasting basis should identify not only the real buyer, but also the user who makes purchasing decisions. Once the purchase has been made, attitudes to suppliers are shaped and subsequent purchases justified via user-feedback loops. What good is it to a company if it successfully sells its products to a customer once, but fails to obtain any return business because the users reject the product and give it bad reports before the purchasing round begins again? Makers of commercial vehicles have realized that, besides the purchasing committees or the final buyer, truck drivers also play a key role. Their vote often determines whether the Scania or the Volvo gets the better evaluation. This being so, steps are taken to establish direct contact with drivers, and the vehicles (particularly the cabins and the general appearance) are designed to meet their needs. Contented drivers are crucially important to the working atmosphere in any transportation company. It is essential, therefore, to pay just as much attention to the drivers' practical preferences and purchasing criteria as to the customers' economic considerations. The same applies in families: Children today often play a major part in deciding where the family should go on its next vacation or what car should be the family's new conveyance. Studies have shown that 20 percent of all car purchasing decisions are substantially influenced by the children, while more than 30 percent of all furniture purchases are dictated by them. It's hardly surprising, then, that advertising for these products is increasingly taking account of children's influence.

Against this background – and here we are going a little beyond the development of a differentiation strategy – you should make every effort to understand how your customers' purchasing decision-making process actually operates. Who obtains and evaluates the information? What stages does the decision-making process go through? Who is responsible for the final contract? Whom should you try to influence at what stage? In sum, it is essential to identify both the real purchaser and those making the recommendations for the client company. Depending on corporate structure and the existence or otherwise of upper limits on purchases, purchasing committees, buyers, the company owner, or the CEO may all be involved in deciding which forklift truck to buy. Those making recommendations may include forklift-truck drivers and warehouse staff. In the case of family vacations, it is usually the parents who make the purchasing decision, influenced by their children or external advisers.

2. *Understand the customer's value chain and your influence on it.* Good differentiators have a high level of competence with regard to the customer's value chain. They know what is important for the client company and how it earns its money. This is why, at this stage, you have to describe the customer's value chain in some detail and identify the points at which you can realistically exert a positive influence on the value-driving or cost-driving factors. At first glance, it would seem more difficult to do this in the case of end users, since it is not so simple to identify individuals' value chains. Perhaps the most effective approach is to describe the process of purchase, use, and disposal and, in doing so, to link the individual actions taken as the product is purchased, used, and disposed of with the attributes that create utility for the customer (increase in performance or reduction in costs). Table 8.1 shows such a description in the case of a bank providing mortgages for house buyers.

A forklift-truck manufacturer's value chain approximates to that of any other manufacturing company. Opportunities for exerting influence exist in the purchasing and use phases (input and output

	Customer's actions	Value-driving factors	Supplier's actions
Purchase	Information	Transparency/Planning	Competent advice
	Cost estimation	Security	Customer education; provision of financial ready reckoner
	Conclusion of contract	Trust	
Use	Controlling	Security	Early-warning system
	Financial management	Optimization of financing	Quotations for optimizing debt rescheduling
Disposal	Completion of loan repayment	Follow-up advice on asset development and protection; insurance	Proposals for new investment opportunities

Table 8.1: An individual's value chain: The example of a mortgage agreement

logistics, and in production). A family vacation can be broken down into the purchase phase, the vacation proper, and retrospective consideration of the trip. Opportunities exist for travel companies to exert influence in all three phases.

3. *Place the purchasing criteria in rank order.* Ascertain which criteria are decisive in the purchase of the products or services on offer. A distinction should be made here between use criteria (fulfillment of core functionality) and signaling criteria (perception of customer value from the customer's point of view). The criteria thus identified should be assessed in terms of their contribution within the customer's value chain. As a supplier, you must know the performance-enhancing or cost-reducing implications that your products or services may have for the customer. The contribution to value creation can be ascertained by analysis of the value chain, with customer interviews and detailed knowledge of the customer's needs, processes, and industrial logic being the decisive factors.

Can price be a purchasing criterion? No, because nobody buys anything because it has a price attached to it. Basically, utility effects such as performance enhancement or cost reduction are crucial in activating a purchase. When customers state that they bought a product on the basis of its price, what they are really referring to is a minimum price–performance ratio. Even with low-cost products or services, customers expect certain performance effects. They are not, however, prepared to pay high prices in order to obtain that value. Thus, if a company adopts a differentiation strategy, the minimum price–performance ratio should never be ranked in first place by the target customer group.

If a company succeeds in offering its customers unique use criteria, it has introduced into the market a completely new form of customer value. This distinguishes it clearly from the competition. The dimensions of the Smart car constitute a unique differentiating characteristic, since only with this vehicle is it possible to take advantage of very small parking spaces. And to return to the forklift trucks: In the 1990s, a leading manufacturer was puzzled as to why the company was increasingly losing orders to a new competitor. After lengthy investigations, the decisive purchasing criterion turned out to be a radio. The drivers, who were heavily involved in the purchasing process, had a clear preference for the vehicle that had built-in entertainment value. Consequently, they advanced a whole host of reasons why the forklift truck without a radio should be consigned to oblivion. In the case of a forklift truck, the purchasing criteria range from the vehicle's expected useful life, via quality and operational safety, to driver ergonomics. In the case of a family vacation, other criteria come to the fore: an opportunity to switch off completely and not have to bother about anything; supervision for the children; or the chance to outdo friends.

4. *Identify where in your value chain unique opportunities for differentiation exist or could be created.* Can you offer exceptional quality because you have put in place special production processes or use exclusive raw materials? Do you have rights that no other supplier has? Is your location a differentiating competitive advantage that creates uniqueness for you? Do you have an exceptional image? As you can see, the aim at this point is not to analyze the existing or potential offer, but rather to identify distinguishing characteristics in the value chain.

   A detailed analysis of the competition is an essential element of this fourth step, because differentiation is relative. For this reason, you need to ascertain what sources of uniqueness there are among the competition, what is standard in the industry, and where the unique competitive advantages lie in your own value-creation process. In the case of our forklift-truck manufacturer, sources of uniqueness might lie in a dense service network, in a preeminent image, or in the use of a novel technology. A travel company can set itself apart from the competition by the size of its service organization, its customer database, or the level of training among its workforce.

5. *Calculate the costs of available or potential sources of differentiation:* *Differentiation has its price.* The cost-raising effects of the value-driving factors need to be analyzed. Opting for a differentiation strategy is a conscious decision to accept higher costs and, hence, a price premium. In our examples, this means that the forklift-truck manufacturer needs to analyze the cost of maintaining a service network, commissioning prestige advertising, and optimizing production, while the travel company has to carry out the same exercise with regard to its service organization, customer database, and the provision of advanced training for its workforce.

6. *Organize your value-driving activities in such a way that you create the most valuable form of differentiation for the customer relative to the extra cost.* In this sixth step, you begin to develop perceptible differentiation. You know where the sources of your uniqueness lie and you are aware of what is of crucial importance to the customer. It's now time to organize your value-driving activities in such a way as to produce an optimal price–performance ratio for the customer. Differentiation strategies generally rely on offering customers a set of utility-enhancing characteristics. It is not just the excellent service offered by Singapore Airlines that sways customers, but also the airline's image, the facilities in the aircraft, or the marketing signals.

In order to obtain good results here, it makes sense to compare the customer's most important purchasing criteria with the sources of uniqueness. What is important for our customers? Where does our differentiation potential lie? Learn from the examples how the forklift-truck manufacturer and the travel company are able to create optimal, differentiating value added. The forklift-truck maker offers a preventive maintenance service at no cost, which excludes potential errors by virtue of the experience upstream. The vehicles are fitted with an early-warning system, which prevents breakdowns or malfunctions. The marketing draws attention to the unique quality of the product, and those exerting influence are specifically addressed. The products are improved at the purchasing and production stages of the value-creation process. Excellent materials and workmanship ensure that breakdowns and malfunctions are largely avoided, which leads to lower operating costs and extends the vehicles' useful life. For the family going on vacation, the comprehensive service provided by the travel company includes an extensive information pack, the handling of all travel formalities, airport transfers, the provision of house and garden maintenance services during their absence, the best spa and health club facilities and the best child supervision in the market segment, and customized services based on the customer database, the sale of addresses, or an image campaign that positions the travel company as a service leader.

7. *Examine the differentiation strategy for imitability.* In this penultimate step, you should assess the extent to which your chosen strategy can prevail against the competition in the long term. Is there a risk that

rivals will be able to imitate your product without any great expenditure, or bring substitute products to the market? Anyone who has examined the development of e-commerce between 1998 and 2001 will know that a lot of ventures failed because they were easy to imitate. This is why it was critical to occupy a market segment as quickly as possible and achieve a critical mass of customers, who represent sources of uniqueness. The global trading platform eBay is attractive because all buyers and sellers know they will reach a very large number of potentially interested individuals. For this reason, a competitor will find it difficult to build up a new network. An additional hurdle for a potential eBay competitor canvassing for new customers is the individual image that buyers and sellers build up for themselves. On eBay, all market participants' past transactions can be examined, in order that potential traders can assess their trustworthiness. If eBay customers move to the Yahoo! online auction, they revert to being nobodies without a past.

Examination of the forklift-truck manufacturer's differentiation strategy against the risk of imitation or substitution produces the following findings. A preventive maintenance service, provided free of cost, cannot be imitated, because the competition does not have the necessary service network (and it is difficult to build one up). The early-warning system is a unique and patented technology, and is therefore protected for three years. The marketing capabilities can be quickly imitated by competitors, since the company relies on an external advertising agency in developing its marketing concept. On the other hand, product quality as a source of uniqueness is difficult to imitate, since the competition does not have the resources required to make the investments necessary to achieve comparable standards.

Examination of the travel company's differentiation strategy against the same risks of imitation or substitution produces the following findings. The service cannot be imitated in the short term, since the competition does not have the requisite service organization in place. On the other hand, the spa and health club facilities and child supervision can be easily copied, and do not therefore constitute a lasting competitive advantage. The customer database cannot be copied since it has been built up over 50 years and is protected against pirate copies. The company's image is unique and difficult to imitate.

8. *Reduce costs in those activities that do not impact on the form of differentiation adopted.* Any company that has placed its faith in unambiguously defined differentiating characteristics should concentrate all its powers on the differentiating activities and performance characteristics, and put in place an active cost-reduction strategy in those areas that are not of any importance to customers. Whatever is of no value to customers is of no value to the company either, and costs in those areas must be minimized. For the forklift-truck manufacturer, that might mean not investing any more in design and low fuel consumption, since the latter is already very low anyway. Irrelevant factors that might have cost-reduction potential for the travel company include customers who do not want an entertainment package and, as a consequence, are not involved in any of the visitor programs while on vacation.

How is a focus strategy developed?

In contrast to the broadly based cost-leadership and differentiation strategies, a focus (or niche) strategy is geared towards a clearly delimited, tightly defined market segment. The niche in question is the company's sphere of operations. It is generally defined in terms of the specific problems posed by a clearly identifiable group of customers. Companies that have adopted a focus strategy develop special capabilities and resources in order optimally to satisfy customer requirements in the particular niche concerned. The value chain of such companies is generally narrow, because it is focused on a small number of products and markets. At the same time, these companies frequently seek to incorporate the vast majority and, in many cases, the entirety of their value-generating activities within their value chains. From research, via purchasing, to after-sales service, all activities are located within the niche supplier's organization. At the same time, niche suppliers try to establish as many points of contact as possible with their customers' valued-added process. Here, too, the suppliers' intention is to offer performance-enhancing products in as many phases of the value-generating process as possible. Rather than being offered just a single product (that is, a single contribution to the value-generating process), the target group is offered as extensive a portfolio of solutions as possible.

Such a strategy, which at first sight may appear somewhat theoretical, gives rise in practice to very relevant effects.

- Niche suppliers are "masters" of their own special areas. By concentrating on a particular sphere of application, on specific technologies, or on clearly defined groups of customers, niche suppliers are able to achieve a high level of quality and of process and market competence. Over time, niche suppliers become better and better at what they do.
- All the supplier's energies are focused on a single objective. On the one hand, this constitutes a high-risk strategy; on the other, however, it also brings with it a compulsion to become the undisputed leader in the market segment in question.
- Customers' requirements are optimally satisfied, which in turn gives rise to a high degree of customer loyalty. Exit barriers for customers are extremely high. Close cooperation with customers produces a wide range of different feedback effects (information, suggestions for improvement, organizational interlocking, and many more besides), which further optimize the service provided for the target group.
- The barriers to entry for competitors are raised, because it is difficult, on the one hand, to achieve the leading niche supplier's level of competence and, on the other, to persuade customers to abandon the (supposedly) leading supplier.

Within this niche, a company can operate as both a differentiating and a cost-leading company. In this respect, the development of a focus strategy is a two-stage process, involving:

1. choice of a narrow market segment, for which a well-thought-out approach to market segmentation is necessary
2. implementation of the differentiation or cost-leadership strategy in the niche as soon as another competitor enters the niche.

Time and time again, whether we are dealing with specialist travel services for older people, gyms that have specialized in strengthening people's backs, or manufacturers of dishwashers for hotels and restaurants, such companies stand out by virtue of their high level of market competence and their close organizational links with their customers. In practice, various strategic approaches have emerged for niche-oriented companies, which will be illustrated below by means of several examples. In detail, these approaches are:

- problem analysis
- target-group analysis
- further development and improved imitation
- niche suppliers as a target group.

A focus strategy is dependent on various parameters located at the level of corporate culture, shaped by management's strategic skill, and conditioned by factors in the wider environment outside the firm. Besides a certain willingness to take risks, the cultural success factors include extreme dedication to and passion for the product, and for the problems posed by the target group, in other words an extreme form of customer orientation. For the management of companies that have adopted a focus strategy, it is important to focus neither on too small a market segment nor on a segment likely to remain profitable only for a short period. Companies that rely on fashionable ephemera run the risk that their success in the niche will be short-lived. Furthermore, they must be able to erect barriers to market entry by competitors. They can do this by continuously extending their technological or commercial superiority, actively fostering customer loyalty, or erecting legal barriers by means of patents, for example. A third key factor is the development and extension of specialist competences. Anyone analyzing in detail the success of niche suppliers will discover that such success is frequently dependent on favorable conditions in the wider environment: Competitors fail to spot the potential in a market segment and are not in a position later on to gain a foothold in the market as the second entrant, because the potential of that particular segment is simply too small. Many firms that are now admired as niche companies are in fact the end result of a protracted weeding-out process. Commercial staying power has created unparalleled market leaders that now find themselves in a monopoly-type situation, which they defend through optimal customer care and a high degree of specialization. Thus, luck and fate are important features of the history of many companies in niche markets.

Below, you will see a few examples and some basic starting points for the development and implementation of a focus strategy. Many of the examples are characterized by innovativeness and risk-aware entrepreneurship – qualities that mark out niche suppliers.

Get to grips with problem situations

Intensive analysis of, and a search for solutions to, specific problems that arise for particular groups of customers is an intelligent starting point for finding niches. At a time when the mass market is serviced with standardized products and services, individual solutions frequently get a raw deal. It is here that commercial potential lies. A company adopting a problem-driven approach will be getting to grips with some of the problems that people and organizations have, and for which the solutions on offer are unsatisfactory, if indeed they exist at all. Hence, the emphasis is on the search for the problem, in order subsequently to develop the solution.

It doesn't do Deutsche Bahn, the German national rail company, much good to complain about customers who prefer to have their goods transported by road rather than by rail, on the grounds that the former is more flexible. It would be better to start devising an even more flexible solution to the problem of transporting goods from A to B. There is a fundamental difference between a product-driven and a problem-driven approach: The former is always geared in a one-dimensional way to a particular output, while the latter is open to the customer's diverse needs, opportunities, and problems. If Deutsche Bahn sees the statement "We operate a rail service" as its mission, it will never be open to the complexity of its customers' problems and their real needs. If, on the one hand, it adopts as its mission the slogan "We get you there on time," a completely different dynamic begins to develop, both for the company and its workers. With a clear remit in mind, every effort can be made to identify scope for improvement, while at the same time developing a keen nose for any potential source of solutions to the problem of getting customers' goods to their destinations on time. Below are three examples of how a problem-solving approach has enabled firms to occupy niche markets.

1. *The problem.* What do you do if you have occasional need of a car, but use one so rarely that it would not be worth while buying a car of your own?

   The solution. Join a car-sharing scheme. In exchange for a fixed monthly fee and a deposit, cars can be reserved over the telephone. The necessary documents and the car keys can be picked up from security containers placed at secure locations within the town or city. The Stattauto scheme in Cologne, for example, takes responsibility for getting the cars serviced and repaired, as well as for insuring them. Customers are billed on a monthly basis. The scheme was launched in 1992 with two cars, ten members, and one depot. Ten years later, a total of 95 cars were available at 19 depots throughout Cologne, and around 1,900 people were taking part in the scheme, making the company led by Ulrich Ferber the largest of its kind in Europe. Furthermore, there are 400 fewer vehicles jamming up the streets of Cologne, since one shared car replaces five private cars.

2. *The problem.* What do you do, as a business person, if you are transferred to a new town or city, but do not have any time, any apartment, or, for that matter, any contacts there?

   The solution. Use the Relocation Service, which serves a very homogeneous group of customers. Companies that operate internationally are the main customers of this company, which offers a diverse portfolio of services to support employees relocating to or within Germany. They will look for accommodations, deal with officialdom, choose schools for children, and organize orientation tours through the town or city in order to help new arrivals settle in. The agency's portfolio of services now even includes help with integrating into social life and establishing contacts (for example, through invitations to certain events or admission to certain clubs). The cost of these services is generally borne by employers, since employees making use of the Relocation Service are able to resume their functions within the company considerably more quickly than those left to fend for themselves. Thus, utility is enhanced on both sides.

3. *The problem.* What if you want to transport an elephant to London and the friendly clerk at Federal Express cannot provide any further assistance?

   The solution. Call World Courier. The company occupies an extreme niche in the transportation industry, dispatching items that are difficult to transport, such as elephants or spare parts for machines, all over the world within the shortest possible time. Thus, the company takes only five hours to deliver spare parts from north Germany to Scotland. World Courier's prices are eight to ten times higher than those charged by the major players in the industry, such as UPS, TNT, or DHL, who do not offer these specialist services. However, customers' lower price sensitivity means there is a risk that the major players will try to make incursions into this segment of the market.

Get to grips with particular groups of customers

Identification of a clearly defined market segment must be at the heart of any focus strategy. This observation was made when the strategic principle was first outlined. If you are really going to get to grips with a particular customer group as a prelude to implementing the strategy, the following actions will be required.

1. *Identification of a homogeneous and commercially attractive target group that currently has no specific solutions on offer.* Ask yourself where customer groups are emerging or where the market completely fails to serve certain groups. For example, the gay market is a developing niche market. Travel services, literature, events, and Internet services specially geared to the needs of gays and lesbians are booming. Another factor encouraging the expansion of this niche market is increasing tolerance within society, which means that the marketing can drag itself out of the gutter, and products can be advertised openly and directly. Quite simply, space has been opened up for marketing. The seniors' market is another example that makes it clear that even large markets are frequently ignored by providers. Thus, in Germany there are only two specialist busi-

nesses for the older age groups – in Heidelberg and in Hamburg. The goods on offer range from furniture, via sight and hearing aids, to specialist books, light fiction, health aids, and fitness machines. Seminars and lectures are also part of the program.

2. *The most intensive analysis of the target group's life, needs, and problems.* Many niche suppliers try to service their customers' value chain on as broad a basis as possible. Their aim is not to make a single contribution to the value chain, but rather to make as many value-enhancing contributions as possible. This is why intensive analysis of consumer behavior is of the utmost importance. At this point, however, many niche suppliers go several stages further. In getting to grips with the narrow market segment, they identify a multiplicity of additional potential opportunities. They ask themselves how their customers live, what else is important to them over and above the use of their products, and how, if they are dealing with industrial customers, they can help them optimize their business.

Consider the market for Turkish consumers in Germany. In 1961, the young student Vural Öger was Turkish immigrant number 31 in Berlin. Eight years later in Hamburg, he hit upon the idea of his life when he realized there were no direct fights from Hamburg to Turkey. Although he has now become one of the largest general tour operators in Germany, he was once the person who discovered a genuinely new market. Today a wide range of ever more specialized products and services aimed at Turkish citizens in Germany is emerging, and the growth rates are high. Turkish specialties not available in German supermarkets, but indispensable to Turkish family cooking, are being imported. There is also great potential in specialist insurance products and financial services that help resolve some of the problems that arise for Turkish people returning to their home country when they retire. At the same time, the market for Turkish media products is booming. Whether it be the Berlin radio station Metropol FM or the distribution of Turkish-language daily newspapers throughout Germany, much of what is now taken for granted as a mass market is in fact the result of the strategic development of a niche market.

3. *Specialization within the niche.* A third decisive step is to specialize further within the niche you have identified. Let us take the example

of Sopur, a company that has specialized in high-quality wheel-chairs for disabled athletes and for general patient care. In addition to its differentiation strategy (quality leadership), the company has concentrated on sport for the disabled and the transportation of the sick. It targets a very narrowly defined group of paraplegics in the market for wheelchairs. This group accounts for only about 3.1 percent of the 360,000 wheelchair users in Germany, but it is very homogeneous in being young, sporty, and well suited to projecting a positive image of disabled people to the general public. The company's high-quality products are supported by a very specific communications policy. Some of the elements that are particularly noteworthy in this regard are the positioning of the wheelchair as an individual product, the company's profound commitment to sport for the disabled, and its close links with opinion-formers in rehabilitation centers and clinics.

Develop ideas further or copy them more intelligently

Innovation is the preeminent entrepreneurial discipline; imitation, on the other hand, generally meets with contempt and derision. There is a widespread prejudice against imitators: It is often said that they have no ideas of their own and are unlikely ever to be the best in the market. However, companies that carefully think through how to develop an existing offer may well create for themselves an opportunity to bring an improved range of products or services to the market, particularly in a clearly defined segment. For this reason, it is useful to examine formulas that have become established in a broadly based market and for which therefore demand clearly exists, and then to ask oneself where in this market there might be subsegments or niches, or how a particular formula might be developed to meet the needs of particular target groups. For example, the bicycle courier service Messenger has further developed the niche for such services, which in Berlin is already hotly contested. The company set out to investigate where it might find new target groups and potential new areas of application for the idea of a bicycle courier service. The service portfolio has been extended to include, among other things, picking up shoes from the cobbler or obtaining theater tickets for the evening performance. The vehicle stock has also been extended to include cars, in order not to have to abandon the market for bulky goods and long-distance transportation services to the motorized competition. However, extending a niche is often risky: The strategy becomes diluted and the company moves into another market that it does not understand. It may perhaps be better for a bicycle courier service to stay small and refer customers making inquiries about bulky goods to other companies.

For television stations, music has always been a valuable and important element of their overall programming. For a long time, however, no television channel dared to rely exclusively on music for its programming. Tastes seemed to be too diverse, the various genres too multifarious. And yet, for 20 years now MTV has been meeting the demand from the 15–29 age group for music videos. Even in this niche market, there is room in Germany for two providers. The music channel VIVA was set up to compete with MTV – and has succeeded in its objective. Second entrants, particularly in media markets, try to establish themselves through new concepts, sharper positioning, and a considerable marketing effort. Examples of companies that have adopted such a strategy include the daily newspaper *Financial Times Deutschland*, which competes with the *Handelsblatt*, and the news channel N24, which goes head-to-head with N-TV. An approach of this kind can work, provided there actually is untapped potential in the market and the differentiation is convincing. The news magazine *Focus*, for example, successfully entered a market previously dominated by the venerable warhorse *Der Spiegel*. By concentrating on a different target group, however, the magazine sought to differentiate itself from its long-established competitor. What is more, the market for news magazines makes it possible to reach very large numbers of people in target groups that are very important to the advertising industry. In economically difficult times, on the other hand, narrow market segments occupied by several providers become high-risk environments in which the weaker players are likely to be ruthlessly weeded out.

Further development or advancement as a conceptual approach to the development of focus strategies applies not only to the range of products and services on offer, but also to markets themselves. The key question to ask here is: "How can we occupy other niches with our existing products, services, technologies, resources, or competences?" Kistler AG in Switzerland services many industries with its special sensor technology. The company produces sensors for the crash walls used in car-crash tests, for research on internal combustion engines, and for plastics processing, as well as for biomechanics, machine-tool control, and automotive and aerospace engineering. Kistler has only a marginal share of the total sensor market, since it focuses exclusively on niches. However, the company has developed superior know-how in the tightly defined niche for highly specialized sensor technology that it occupies. Its sensitive sensors are used to detect forces and movements that are too quick for the human eye. The company services the market for specialist applications that are insufficiently profitable and too complicated for large-volume producers, such as the bioplatforms used in sports like weightlifting, the high jump, and the long jump to provide highly accurate measurements of force progression. Renker is another company that has extended its client industry portfolio, with its special coatings technology that is used in paper and foil processing. This technology is applied to products as diverse as lampshades, satellites, thermal paper for fax machines and cash registers, windows in both buildings and cars, and plastic films for the automotive and aerospace industries. Besides the characteristic qualities of customer-driven niche providers (rapid reaction to market requirements, intensive nurturing of customer contacts, a user advisory service, and a highly flexible sales and distribution system), the company must be permanently on the lookout for new areas of application for its own technology.

The following steps are necessary if you are to develop your range of products or services intelligently.

1. Describe your offer in one sentence.
2. List your most important competitors and thoroughly examine the range of products or services they provide. Describe the existing offer.
3. Divide the market into segments.
4. Identify the most important requirements of each individual segment.
5. Identify the weaknesses of the existing offer, particularly as they apply to each individual segment.
6. Develop a better offer for each individual segment. How can you put in place an optimal range of products or services for segment XYZ by changing the differentiating factors, such as quality, service, equipment and facilities, technological standards, flexibilization, minimal costs, environmental friendliness, and design?

Become the specialist's specialist or the extremist's extremist

One of the most striking things to emerge from an analysis of niche suppliers is that many companies have, in turn, identified niche suppliers as their customers. In this sense they are, as it were, specialists for specialists. For example, the Munich company Arnold & Richter Cine Technik, established in 1917, has an outstanding reputation in the market for movie cameras. It focuses not on the market as a whole, but on providing equipment for the most demanding professional moviemakers. The company supplies technically sophisticated, computer-controlled 35mm cameras and has a 60 percent market share in this global niche. The Arriflex, 1,000 of which are produced annually, is a byword for excellence among directors worldwide. The prominent position occupied by the company's founders, August Arnold and Robert Richter, was underlined in 1982, when they were awarded an Oscar for their revolutionary life's work. The company has received nine Oscars for technical innovations since 1996.

Forplan has established itself in the business consultancy industry as a specialist's specialist by focusing on consultancy services for public and private rescue services. Although the company is very small compared with the large business consultants, its high degree of specialization has enabled it to capture around 80 percent of the rescue-services market.

These examples reveal two problematical aspects of focus strategies.

- Unilateral dependency can lead to the whole basis of a business simply collapsing when an industry goes through structural change or crisis. What happens if the movie industry is afflicted by a global crisis or a technological innovation takes Arnold & Richter's cameras completely out of the running?
- It is important that a niche provider has a high level of competence in servicing its particular market segment that cannot easily be copied by other suppliers. In the case of Forplan, the company's detailed knowledge of the needs of rescue services is the crucial factor that prevents it being replaced by standard, undifferentiated consultancy services.

Observe the basic rule for focus strategies

The principles for implementing a focus strategy can be summarized as follows: You should be catering for an existing or latent need that is not adequately satisfied by any of the suppliers currently operating in the market. You need a clear, focused definition of the niche target group, whose needs structure should be as homogeneous as possible. You should be the first to enter the market segment in question, and build up your position as an innovator as rapidly as possible. Ascertain whether the niche factor can be applied to different industries or target groups. Develop superior know-how with regard to the niche factor as it applies to the original tightly defined market segment. Defend your special position and safeguard your technological superiority. Keep your products and services exclusive, and take active steps to keep your customers loyal.

The contribution made by developing a business strategy within the framework of the strategic process: The functional areas, such as marketing, human resource management, sales, production, or R&D, now have clear specifications for the end product and everything associated with it. Although decisions taken at departmental level are often relatively abstract in nature, they are, nevertheless, an indispensable aid for the individual functions within a company as they seek to guide and coordinate their activities.

9. Developing Functional Strategies

What you need to do when developing functional strategies (Figure 9.1):The development of functional strategies represents the first step towards the implementation phase. The level of explicit detail increases, and you start to get down to work. This is the latest point at which the conceptual and planning statements of the business unit strategy should be replaced by clear functional policies: from planning to action. Here we will explore as examples two functional areas, so as to describe the integrated nature of strategy development.

The business unit strategy provides a general orientation as to how competitive advantages can be developed. However, specific sets of measures for effective implementation of these business unit strategies are first formulated at the functional level. The management team thus describes in terms of a step-by-step plan the operational consequences resulting from the corporate strategy and the business unit strategy for the individual functions. The functional strategy is therefore a bridge to implementation, because the level of planning detail is increased and specific action instructions are given. The links between the three strategy levels will be illustrated below, on the basis of overviews of the decision-making in two important functions. These two functions are human resource management and marketing/sales, whose most important activities will be presented. Specialists in these particular areas will forgive us if at this point we cannot go into great detail. The aim is to persuade the management teams of these functions to plan long-term and to start thinking about implementation of the business strategy. In most cases, the horizontal coordination between the functions can be greatly improved as a result. If only the salespeople and the R&D specialists could understand each other better!

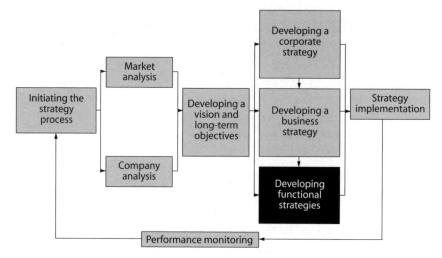

Figure 9.1: Developing functional strategies as the eighth stage of the process

How is a marketing strategy developed?

Often a contrast is drawn between operational and strategic marketing. In operational marketing, decisions are taken primarily concerning the product characteristics, the price, the promotion, and the distribution channels. Strategic marketing, by comparison, comes very close to strategic management, as it is presented in this book. As distinct from business unit strategy, the marketing expert translates the general targets and quantitative plans to a higher level of detail.

Select your target market

The decisions of operational marketing are made on the basis of a very thorough analysis of the market and, in particular, of the customer groups. What are looked for are homogeneous market segments that are large enough to sell the particular products and services at a profit. Markets can be divided into segments according to many different criteria. Once market-segment boundaries are defined, this has far-reaching consequences for the organization of the business units and for the differentiation of the offer made in the individual segments. Often companies give in to inducements to move across the segment boundaries. For example, a plant constructor, in the interests of customer retention, can manufacture machines for a good customer that are not part of the standard product range. Or a hard-working salesperson offers to smaller firms products that have actually been tailored to large companies. For the target markets define exactly who is responsible for the purchase decision and how this can be influenced. As with the portfolio analysis of departments, product groups or individual products can also be arranged in a life cycle. An enhanced understanding of the level of maturity of the markets improves your ability to make a prognosis of market development and face up to further marketing decisions.

Define the product characteristics

The product characteristics are defined in terms of the basic strategy. If you pursue a strategy of differentiation, you will then be attempting to satisfy the desires and expectations of the purchaser in the best possible manner. In the first instance, price is of secondary importance. Cost leadership is attained if the product characteristics are determined not primarily with the customer, but with the production team. Product characteristics are defined in terms of the following attributes, among others: design, functionality, size, reliability, packaging, degree of individual adaptation, labeling, and service. From the mix of these characteristics, a product is generated that stands out positively from the competition and, at the same time, extends the existing product range without cannibalizing it as far as possible.

Select the distribution channels

Which selling channels reach the selected market segment in the most effective manner? How selectively, exclusively, or intensively should a sales channel be used? How great is the bargaining power of the potential sales partner? How can the sales and distribution partners be motivated and monitored? Which distribution partners have the necessary competences and product know-how to sell our products? What profit margin must be paid to the partners in each case? How high are the costs for control of the distribution system? On the basis of these questions, you will decide on a mix of sales channels: an individual store, a large store, your own sales team, independent representatives, online sales, catalogue sales, or store-in-store concepts.

Define the advertising strategy

The function of the advertising strategy is defined on the basis of a clear customer analysis. It can serve to inform the customer about the product, to satisfy a purchase need, or to transform a clearly identified need into a purchase. Advertising activities increase customer loyalty and can have the effect of raising the frequency of product use. "Pull" advertising strategies are directed at moving the customers towards the locations where your product is being sold. In television advertisements, the customer is strongly recommended to visit the next Ford or Mercedes dealer. "Push" advertising strategies are directed at motivating the sales channels to sell more of your product. Thus, brewers using direct sales methods can motivate pubs and bars to sell their brand of beer, or can even threaten to stop deliveries if a certain volume is not sold. Among sportswear manufacturers, for example, marketing has for a long time become a central business activity alongside R&D. In the case of Puma, Nike, Adidas, or Reebok, marketing activities account for 10–15 percent of turnover. With this volume of activity, it is important to measure the effective influence of advertising measures on turnover. Ask those responsible for your marketing how large the increase in turnover would be if the advertising budget were to be doubled.

Define the price level

The decision as to how high the price of the product should be influences the marketing mix. Thus, low-priced products, for example, require other sales channels. The pricing decision is influenced by a number of factors. On the one hand, there are psychological prices, such as $299, which have a positive effect on consumers. Prices that are above average can also have a positive effect on consumers, since they generate an important signal: "Things that don't cost anything are worth nothing." Häagen-Dasz has toyed with the slogan "Everything gets more expensive. We remain so." The company has thereby positioned itself at the pinnacle of the premium ice-cream brands. A second method of calculation is to work out the total costs of manufacturing the product and add on the desired profit margin. Or you can attempt to evaluate, via your customers, the value placed on your product and take this as an indicator for the end price. Often, however, competitors dictate the selling price, and there is no alternative other than to match it, if you are basically unable to differentiate yourself from the competition. With high-tech products in particular, innovative products are introduced into the market with very high margins in order to finance the innovation activity (skimming). Capacity bottlenecks can also be controlled by means of price. Depending upon the price elasticity of the customer, some will move across to a competitor product in the event of a price rise. For that reason, companies often have the problem of matching together growth in turnover and good margins.

What are the tasks of personnel management?

In general, it is regularly stated that the employees are the most important resource of the company. In many companies, though, such statements are nothing more than effective lip service paid to the job market. Or to put it another way: How many top managers do you know have started their career in the personnel department? How many heads of personnel do you know either are not represented on the board or do not have any weight there? Granted, heads of personnel often do not have a very good understanding of the business operation, and simply cannot converse on the subject. Often, they are condemned to implementing the strategies of their colleagues in top management in a purely reactive manner. Strategic personnel management can, however, mean that a professional estimation of the knowledge and competences of the employees is used decisively to influence the competitive strategy (in an "inside-out" manner).

Plan the personnel requirement proactively

Personnel planning can be reactive to queries from the reporting hierarchy, or to an analysis of future strategic requirements and the necessary employee profiles that are linked with these. The aim is to
populate future vacant or new positions with the correct employees.
Planning of this kind is based on a detailed analysis and design of job
requirements. Often the job profiles are assembled into categories.
These then form, together with the assessment of individual profiles,
the basis for the calculation of the fixed-pay component.

Recruiting: Increase your attractiveness as an employer

Personnel recruitment is a central task of the personnel department.
Vacant positions can either be filled through the internal personnel
market (by employee movements) or through the external job market.
Here, both markets must be developed intensively on a long-term
basis. Most of the larger companies have communication media that
can serve the internal job market: bulletin boards, the house newspaper, or the intranet. In the external job market, newspaper advertisements, university recruiting, or the immediate enticement of a
candidate via personal contacts are the usual instruments. The most
urgent and delicate searches for qualified personnel are often turned
over to headhunters, executive search companies, or employment
agencies. In times of economic difficulty, a further option for the filling
of vacant positions usually becomes more unpopular: "body leasing."
Managers or staff temporarily perform the work required at significantly higher costs on the basis of hourly or daily rates.

Personnel selection: Produce your mix of methods

The selection method should increase the probability that the candidate will be successful in the new position. Consultants such as
McKinsey or BCG are able to sift out the majority of applicants on the
basis of their résumés, statements of personal motivation, references,

and education and employment records. Often bad mathematics reports during time in high school, or a lack of out-of-school activities, are sufficient to make the decision. If candidates clear this hurdle, they are invited to what is usually a one-day "interview experience": in the morning three interviews, with an intermediate selection at midday, and, for those remaining, another two or three interviews in the afternoon. The interviews are usually conducted by a senior consultant. McKinsey sometimes check whether the candidates have "drive" (that is, whether they achieved something in their lives), how they react in the social environment, and whether they have analytical skills. These analytical skills appear to be particularly important, since usually the largest part of the time is devoted to solving case studies or abstract thinking tasks: "How many fuel stations are there in Germany?" "How many couples will tie the knot in Switzerland in 2005?" "Why are the access-point covers to sewers round?" With these questions, it is not primarily about estimating correctly (as long as one does not misjudge the answers by a factor of 10 or more). What really matters is the analytical decomposition of the problem.

Other organizations, such as Effem Mars, Credit Suisse, or the Swiss Army, are devoted to a combination of individual interviews, psychological tests, and, finally, an assessment center. In the case of Effem Mars, the eight candidates are placed in artificial work situations. They are alternately observed as a group and individually by four supervisors, and evaluated on the basis of a list of criteria. After each group exercise, the candidates must assess each other and then produce a ranking list. Now and again, they must place themselves in the top two, since they know that out of the eight candidates only two will receive a contract of employment. Assessment centers can be used both for internal as well as for external selections. The last hurdle is often a health check by doctors.

Personnel assessment: Have the courage to give open and sound feedback

In most companies, there are positions that provide for a variable salary component on the basis of performance. It is mainly the sales-people who get a bonus on the basis of sales figures. These are relatively easy to establish. If, however, qualitative assessment features enter into the situation, objective evaluation becomes more difficult. How would you assess the work of a journalist or a university teacher? How are mechanical engineers to be assessed? Department heads usually do not have answers to these questions – but they are able to produce a ranking list of their employees and can immediately say who are the best. This shows that intuitive assessment criteria are being used. Have the courage to make this intuition explicit, and to agree objectives and standards with the employees, monitor these periodically, and give open and clear feedback.

Bonus or penalty? That is seldom the question. Naturally it is easier to pay out bonuses, when your employees' children go to the same school as your own, and you might meet each other at the supermarket on a Saturday. Supervisors are often amazingly averse to conflict where assessment discussions are concerned. Even when the assessment is not linked to a monetary bonus, supervisors have a duty to form a picture during the year of their employees' performance, and to provide feedback to them. The annual feedback discussion should not, then, be any kind of surprise for the employees, and should not only relate to the months of November and December. Collect evidence of performance regularly, and sometimes communicate to the employees your estimation of their performance spontaneously. Prepare for the annual conversation with each employee carefully, and obtain from the employees a self-assessment of their performance.

Personnel development: Identify possible futures

The quality of personnel-development schemes is often an important point in the selection of an employer. Personnel-development tasks include the organization of internal or external further-training seminars, and the identification of long-term career plans. Imagine what happens if an internal assessment center is set up, but the best receive no new challenges for a number of years. The assessment, selection, and development of personnel are strongly linked together. There is also little sense if, in the employee assessment at the end of the year, deficiencies in presentation skills are established, but no suitable further-training measures are decided upon and implemented.

A further problem area in personnel development is the filling of international positions. In many companies, it is part of an all-around career to have proved oneself in another country. However, the network of company contacts enjoyed by these highfliers often gets thinner as a result of the time spent abroad, and when they return they find that there is no suitable challenge open to them. Personnel development can, in addition, provide various services such as the coaching of leadership skills, team-development sessions, or particular specialist seminars. The marketability of the personnel-development areas is fostered by clear internal cost accounting for their services, and the competition provided by external bodies.

The contribution made by developing functional strategies within the framework of the strategic process: The functional areas have developed clear strategic approaches and have agreed these with each other. Often interface management and the orchestration of functional activities are important sources of enduring competitive advantage.

10. Strategy Implementation

What you need to do when implementing strategy (Figure 10.1): During the strategic process, you have always been thinking about the implementation phase. You have selected the participants accordingly, and assessed strategic alternatives according to their prospects of implementation. At this point it is now all about setting up strategic projects. We have chosen the word "project," and should now define this clearly. Projects have a person in charge, a project team, resources, and milestones. You now have the difficult task of modifying the organizational structures and processes, the people, and the company culture so that they match up to the strategy selected.

Changes are usually associated with strong emotions, and demand modifications to individual custom and practice. Such routines are important to ensure that the day's business is carried out efficiently. The larger and older the organization, however, the more difficult it is to alter these routines. Just think about your routine activities each morning. You clean your teeth, wash your face, or take a shower. Now make a deliberate attempt to alter some of these routines, without sticking a note on the mirror to remind you. Clean your teeth with your other hand, or before you shower rather than afterwards. Even after several attempts, most people do not succeed in reminding themselves to alter the order of these routines spontaneously. Changes need a certain psychological pressure from outside if they are actually to be put into effect. It is particularly difficult in successful companies to achieve a broad consensus that a need for action exists. How can such a pressure for action be built up?

Change is introduced if either the pressure exerted by the forces for change (such as alterations to the technological state of the art) is raised, or the barriers opposing change (such as poor information, mistrust, or a risk-averse culture) are dismantled. Raising the pressure

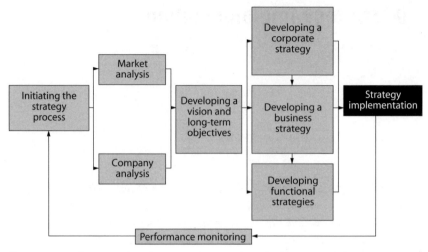

Figure 10.1: Strategy implementation as the ninth stage of the process

for change often leads to an increase in resistance, and can therefore be a zero-sum game. The recommendation must therefore be that the barriers opposing change are identified accurately and purposefully dismantled. Organizations can accordingly be modified in a three-stage process: "Unfreeze – Move – Refreeze" (Lewin 1963).

This is an easy principle to understand, but is difficult to implement. In the first phase (unfreeze), staff should be encouraged to consider their own patterns of procedure critically. Why do we decide to give up smoking on January 1st, rather than August 13th? We need a point at which we can say that one chapter is closed, and we want to open up a new one. A radical alteration to workplace conditions, or a move into new offices, can create such an effect. Only when a large part of the organization is ready for change can the alterations be pursued in a purposeful manner (move). Although the maxim "Change is the only constant in today's world" enjoys general acceptance, fundamental changes to processes and procedures should be regarded as complete when a certain period of time has elapsed. Perceived achievements are applauded, and once again work can start on developing the routines necessary for dealing with day-to-day happenings (refreeze).

Another way of gaining the organization's full attention is to engender a crisis deliberately. A feeling of security often predominates, particularly in large companies: "Those people at company headquarters will simply have to release a bit more money if things aren't going so well for us at the moment." Or even more difficult to deal with: "Everything's going fine for us – why do we need to change?" Shaking up the organization by means of shock tactics can make the employees ready to accept initiatives for change. Obviously, it is inadvisable to resort to these tactics too often, or to scare already intimidated and insecure staff even further.

Provocation of a sense of crisis can often be achieved most rapidly by the use of actual figures from (poor) sets of company accounts, by direct feedback from unsatisfied customers, or by warnings concerning the increasing strength of the competition. It can also, however, be sufficient to show a five-minute time-lapse video of a map of the geography of the Roman Empire, and to observe how a great empire can arise over a period of more than four minutes, only later to fall apart in a few seconds. After that, most managers are able to talk through examples of companies such as AEG or Encyclopaedia Britannica.

To make it more credible that the company must move away from the status quo, old status symbols relating to past successes should be removed. Company cars with chauffeurs, luxuriously fitted executive offices, or the business lounge for top management – all give the staff the feeling that everything is ok. To produce fundamental change in a company and to implement far-reaching strategic initiatives, it is insufficient simply to scratch the surface and draw up new organization charts. Processes of change frequently operate as in the following example. Imagine a large tree in wintertime. A huge number of rooks are sitting on the tree and are happily settled. An angry farmer now tries to drive the rooks away by shooting up at the tree with a shotgun. Whereupon the rooks fly up, circle over the tree, and return after a few minutes. Most of them are sitting on different branches, and a few rooks lie dead on the ground. To prevent the process of change from operating in this manner, you must plan from the very beginning to make a deep incision into the company's value system.

At what levels can you influence initiatives for change?

When the basic strategic orientation is set, four levels of operation must be aligned to this orientation: the organizational structure, the various organizational systems, the employees, and the organizational culture. As far as the time axis is concerned, modifications to the structure are relatively quick to bring about, whereas new systems require months or even years to be implemented. However, making changes to people, and any linked changes to the culture of the organization, requires much longer. Studies have shown that – depending upon the size and the age of the company – some traces of the old organizational culture can still be present after one generation (that is, after some 25 years). As soon as a company is formed, certain cultural courses are set that are not at all easy to change later on. Plan for cultural change with a long time horizon, therefore, and develop a certain tolerance to frustrations if it all takes a bit longer than planned.

Change the structure

The negative example of the tree with the rooks shows that while structural changes can be carried out very quickly, they often achieve little apart from generating unrest. Structural changes should therefore be focused on the implementation of strategic initiatives, as expressed by the maxim "Structure follows strategy." As with most rules this one also has exceptions. After any fundamental change of the organizational structure, the "refreeze" phase, that is, the development of efficient processes, should not be destroyed by a new bout of far-reaching changes. The organizational structure can thus be prescribed for one or two years as a framework for development of the strategy.

Changing structures does not only mean drawing up new organization charts, but also modifying the job descriptions that are affected. How high should the level of decentralization of activities be? How flexible should the organization be? Which new tasks are necessary? Which activities can be performed by external suppliers? How much decision-making freedom should the individual units have, so that they can trade as business units, but nevertheless in the interests of the whole company? A job description provides a definitive written record in a uniform format of the organizational integration of a post, its objectives, activities, competences, and responsibilities, as well as its relationship with other posts.

Change the systems

Which new capabilities are needed to implement the strategy? How should the information flows or the material flows be organized? How should the strategic- and operational-planning system look? How are the budget rounds to be configured? How can incentive systems, assessment systems, or control systems purposefully influence the behavior of employees, and direct activities into the correct channels? Good systems can propel employees into certain modes of behavior. If the salespeople, for example, do not build up stores of customer data, and do not write any customer reports, intelligent software solutions can provide the answer that enables qualitative and quantitative monitoring of data entered. Naturally it will not be easy to introduce a new sales system – even if it only means one additional form per customer visit. As with all initiatives for change it is not possible to develop patent remedies that will work for all occasions. However, in general the systems should be simple, display clear benefits, and be interlinked. In a very short space of time, Ford was able to reduce its suppliers' defect rates to zero by a simple system change that formed part of a business-reengineering project. Even if only part of the delivery was defective or incomplete, the complete delivery was turned back at the factory gates. Moreover, since the employees were unable to bypass the new system (there was no option for securing an incomplete or defective order), the suppliers were educated into the zero-defect culture within a very short period of time.

Thus, a new system could, for example, relieve the sales team of certain tasks, such as the writing of Christmas cards, and thereby motivate them to maintain customer data. Customer data can also be generated by a system that enables salespeople to use their cellphones to record their impressions of discussions with customers on an endless answering machine. The results are then evaluated by a member of staff back in the office and made available to everybody. Also negative incentives, for example, payment of travel expenses only after a full customer report has been completed, can be helpful in certain circumstances.

An important system for the intensification of changes is the bringing-together of employee evaluations and salaries. Many companies introduced the 3P system for staff salaries a long time ago.

Person. One component of the fixed salary is determined by the individual profile of the employee: age, experience, training, and so on.

Position. The second component of the fixed salary is determined by the job that is being undertaken: responsibility for staff, responsibility for turnover or costs, required qualifications. Analysis of the jobs and the creation of job categories (jobs with the same weighting) can prove to be a difficult and politically explosive exercise.

Performance. In addition to the fixed salary, a variable proportion of the salary is being paid out, to an increasing extent, in recognition of performance achieved. To give this bonus an effective weighting, it should not be less than 10 percent, and can lead to a salary that is wholly dependent upon success (as is the case for some top managers such as Steve Jobs of Apple). The current debate as to whether any such bonus should be tied to individual, group, or company objectives can be solved by means of a healthy mix of all components. It is important that discussions to agree objectives provide a clear starting position for an assessment of performance that is as objective as possible.

Change the people

What know-how and experience must the employees bring with them to be able to implement the strategy successfully? Who are the key people who can effect initiatives for change? What expectations do the employees have and how can they be motivated? Radical processes of change often begin with the replacement of top management. As in a soccer team, the replacement of the trainer can be an important symbol and can provide new stimuli. While the modification of a company's "genetic code" can indeed achieve some rapid effects, it is also associated with a number of costs. In addition to the financial aspects of salary payouts, much knowledge is lost that can only be reconstructed with difficulty. Usually, however, a company's need for change is not linked with individual people. Further education measures, the formation of a dedicated and mutually complementary management team, and the selection of the right people for corresponding strategic tasks are central planks of the implementation of strategic initiatives.

Change the culture

The organizational culture can be defined as a value system that has been built up through experience and is manifested in common modes of behavior and organizational routines. It is transferred by means of company symbols and anecdotes to new generations. Here a differentiation can be made between three cultural planes (Schein 1984).

1. *Visible artifacts* such as clothing, office equipment, social etiquette, architecture, cafeteria meals, documentation, ceremonies, or pieces of art exhibited.
2. *Articulated value statements* concerning aspects of our life. This plane of the organizational culture is often to be found in mission statements, management principles, dogmas, action maxims, ideologies, or images of company heroes.
3. *Unarticulated basic assumptions* concerning fundamental facets of life form the third component of the culture. In one cultural group, for example, time is described using the metaphor of the sea (time is like water in the sea: That which is not used today is still there tomorrow) whereas in another cultural group the comparison with a river is preferred (time is like water in a river: That which is not used today is lost forever).

It takes a long time to change the company culture. Arie de Geus of Shell once remarked that the last source of an ongoing competitive advantage is to be looked for in the company's learning culture. Sources of ongoing competitive advantage have four characteristics: They are valuable, rare, hard to imitate, and hard to substitute. A positive learning culture is one of the few areas to fulfill these four criteria. The learning culture is difficult to imitate for at least two reasons.

First, it is difficult to describe – or how would you describe your company culture? A first step towards modification of the culture requires clear descriptions of today's culture and how it should appear in the future. These should not be equated with vague mission statements. The culture should be exemplified by the lives of top management. Staff should exchange company anecdotes on what is meant by customer orientation, professional project management, and transparency.

Second, the learning culture is difficult to imitate, because culture can only be modified over a long period of time. Symbolic actions can help to make clear to staff how they should behave in the future. Thus, a desperate head of sales attempted to motivate his salespeople to spend four out of five working days with customers. His people preferred not to travel, however, but to spend four out of five days in the office. After several verbal admonishments, he took hammer, nails, and strips of wood, and nailed up the doors to their offices. Action of this kind certainly provides material for discussion, gives food for thought, and probably modifies behavior patterns too.

How can processes of change be managed?

After we have thought about the initiation and general structure of initiatives for change, the question arises as to how in fact processes of change can be managed in a positive manner. As already stated, there are no patent remedies for this. This is not just a cheap excuse, but a warning against waging war on all sides and against an unreflective application of methods that have been successful in other companies. In your company, there are also various subcultures that reflect allegiances of geography, religion, or subsidiary companies.

*Determine exactly the timing and intensity of initiatives
for change*

After you have decided which of the four elements you must change so as to be able to implement your strategic initiatives, you must start to

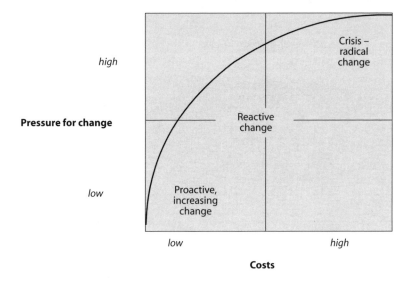

Figure 10.2: Costs as a function of pressure for change

think about the point in time and the intensity of initiatives for change. As Figure 10.2 shows, the costs incurred are dependent upon the point in time at which the changes are initiated, and on their intensity. By means of a proactive change management of small steps, it may be possible to save costs. If the pressure for change from the external environment is low, it is correspondingly difficult to alter the company very fundamentally. As we know from the classification of the strategic themes, these should be identified early on and contingency plans should be developed before things come to a crisis. Unfortunately this is not always possible (see the change of successful companies).

Concentrate on the change of the organization's layer of clay: The middle-management level

If, in some kind of crisis situation, change must happen quickly, the decision-making processes often have to be temporarily centralized, with dictatorial commands coming from above. Democratic bottom-up changes require too much time. Many Japanese management teams

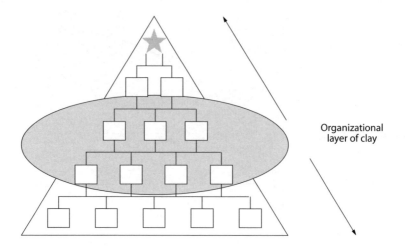

Figure 10.3: The organizational layer of clay

see the crucial area for change not in top management, but at the middle-ranking management levels. The term "organizational layer of clay" expresses the fact that in companies there is a layer that blocks off initiatives from above and below (Figure 10.3). In the same way as water cannot penetrate a layer of clay, good ideas and information cannot pass through the organization's "layer of clay."

For this reason, it is worth anchoring fundamental changes securely in middle management. Identify the draft horses of organizational change. Take care to ensure that these get the necessary support to form a dominant coalition in their areas, and that they can call on enough influence to make painful decisions and carry them through. It may perhaps be preferable to limit an initiative for change to part of the company in the first instance. If this is successful, you will have a much easier task ahead of you in the other areas.

Consider strategy implementation to be a portfolio of projects

Strategic implementation projects often start as a three-lane highway and end as a narrow field path. Sometimes it is part of the old company culture to allocate longer-term projects a lower priority than customer projects. The failure of a strategy project can also be explained in terms of the dynamic environment or the lack of time available alongside the daily business. For this reason, it is recommended that a full-time project leader be appointed for larger strategy projects. If after three to four months no fundamental decisions or strategy alternatives have yet been tabled, it is a sign of lack of project management or the paralysis caused by too much analysis. Our advice: Use similar project-management standards for both your strategic activities and your customer-oriented projects. A project is a series of interdisciplinary time-limited activities that are linked together for the achievement of a specific objective or end result.

Characteristic features of a project. Projects have a customer, a steering committee, a project leader, and a project team; a clearly formulated and signed contract; a start point, intermediate objectives, and an end point; planning specifications and framework conditions, a number of areas of authority involved, and an ongoing "required/actual" set of comparisons.

Activities within the project. General activities during a project include: scoping the problem and the task, achieving agreement between objectives and procedure, goal-oriented planning and use of resources, monitoring and control of the project progress, project marketing, and leadership of the project group.

Relevant questions. Why has the project been set up (general objectives)? What must be achieved (specific project aims)? How should it proceed (ways and means)? Where is the project to be worked on (project site)? Who is affected by the project (groups concerned)? When will it be started and concluded (schedule-planning)? How much is the project costing (project costs)? How good must the results be (quality)?

If the implementation of strategic objectives is seen as a portfolio of projects, this can also prevent resources being allocated in an unrealistic manner. Often the production of an analysis or the implementation of an idea is expected to happen in addition to the daily workload, something that endangers the whole of the strategy implementation.

Configure the political processes

Seen from a structural perspective, organizations are determined by objectives set from the top and by a corresponding set of policies. However, a strategy will never function without the power factor. Projects can be motivated by the influence of power. Management has, in fact, the duty to mobilize people by the exertion of power.

Strategic decision processes usually bring about a time of meager resources. Conflicts in the decision-making processes are a natural and necessary element, since differences in values, preferences, and perceptions always exist between individuals and groups. By means of these conflicts, the status quo is questioned and renegotiated. Power is a central factor to solve such conflicts. Organizational systems of objectives mostly arise out of a negotiation process between different power groups or coalitions.

The source of power can be very variable. The position in the organization's hierarchy can give a manager the power to give instructions, to reward or punish. Often experts have a strong power base as a result of their very special knowledge, and exploit this in meetings through the deliberate use of technical terms. Also, one comes across charismatic leader personalities, although much less often than is generally assumed. In meetings in which strategic objectives are being discussed, such power bases show to best advantage, and must somehow or other be directed onto the right paths.

Principle of reversed action. Often one does not realize that power is being exerted. Are there differences in the way in which discussions are held that depend upon whether the head comes to your office to see you, or you go to their office? Also, the order of seating in a meeting, or subtle gestures and comments, can have a strong influence on those taking part. To disclose such power processes, you can ask yourself whether the action that has just occurred could also have occurred in the other direction. The boss slaps you on the shoulder and says, "You've done that well." Would you praise your boss generously and slap them on the shoulder in this manner? Can you unpack what the boss was actually trying to say? If the answer is yes, a power equilibrium exists.

Power management in meetings. The first challenge is to recognize where and how power operates. Only after this has been achieved can one attempt to manage power processes. Here, methods that have been known about for a long time can help: the nomination of a devil's advocate, the distribution of group or individual activities, or the advice to the boss that they should be the last to speak on a subject. It can be very worth while to spend half an hour on one occasion defining the rules for discussion in the management team meetings, and then to hang these on the wall where everyone can see them. If this is insufficient to create a well-balanced flow of conversation, the following exercise can help.

Disciplined discussions. For this exercise, the moderator prepares three times four different playing cards for each participant in the discussion (maximum of ten). Each card has a different color and function. If a participant in the discussion plays a green C card, this entitles them to a comment that builds on the argument of the previous speaker. The yellow N card introduces a new argument. The black Q card entitles the previous speaker to ask a question. Finally, the red A card allows the discussion to be analyzed at a fundamental level. In many groups, it can make sense to introduce the additional rule that each card only entitles the owner to speak for a limited period of time. Each participant in the discussion receives three cards of each kind. Now select a strategically important subject for discussion and make sure that the rules are followed. After about 20 minutes, you will note that the intensity is winding down, and it is time to break off from the experiment. Some of those who have a lot to say will have no cards left, while others will be sitting there with a complete set. Now discuss the following questions with the group: How did you feel during the discussion? What are the advantages of structuring discussions in this way? On the basis of this experience, what rules for discussion should be held on to in future meetings – even without cards?

Match your change management to the company situation: The special case of turnaround management

One talks about a turnaround if a company has been brought back from a situation of deep crisis to a profitable state. Privatizations, in which organizations have been led out of the security of the public sector into the raw reality of competition (for example, the rail or postal services), often display similar characteristics. Usually, it can be observed that such a process occurs in two phases.

Restructuring. A company that is doing well, a newly formed company, or a company in a turnaround situation – each needs a different type of manager to lead it. Therefore, a suitable turnaround manager is first of all sought, who will concentrate on forming a powerful management team that can carry through change. Turnaround managers look for areas in which they can quickly produce success, in order to win the trust of the interest groups. Transparent controlling instruments are introduced to be able to build a reliable navigation system for management decisions. The balance is restructured. In the event of layoffs, a social plan and retraining measures must be provided for the employees. Activities that do not belong to the core business are sold where possible. The organization chart is redeveloped, and the core processes are checked for fitness for purpose and modified where necessary. This phase should be completed after one to two years.

Growth. The company is now lean and ready to start to grow again slowly. Building on the core competences, the company can again set itself on a course for expansion. Decision capabilities are once again delegated downwards, and the organizational culture slowly starts to change. Messages signaling success show the company that it is on the right path, and motivate the employees. New interesting posts are created and the image of the company improves. Once again, an above-average level of investment is put into marketing. Penetration of the home market increases, and this stable position allows the company to develop new products and markets.

The contribution made by strategy implementation within the framework of the strategic process: Companies need success stories. And this is exactly what this phase should provide. Of course, strategic projects sometimes fail, and a company culture cannot always be fundamentally altered in two years. As a result of this phase, it is, however, essential to show that the organization is on the right path and that the effort is proving worth while. Evidence of this kind is then collected, when the strategic process cycle is closed and the phase of performance measurement is reentered.

Summary: Process is Much More Important than Content

Before you go back to the day-to-day business of your company, we would like to encapsulate our prime ideas in one sentence: "Configure the processes with patience, realism, and determination, and you will see that the contents automatically gain in quality." We are convinced that development and implementation of a strategy for most managers do not pose an intellectual problem, but rather a problem of mental attitude. It is not particularly difficult to understand how a SWOT analysis or a sensitivity analysis works. You don't need an MBA to be able to draw a value chain. On the contrary, the simpler the strategic tools, the more successful the ideas in practice. Stephen Covey's bestseller *The 7 Habits of Highly Effective People* describes in simple terms how individuals can increase their effectiveness. Basic principles such as "first things first" are so simple that, from many readers, they elicit a slightly sarcastic "First things first – why didn't someone tell me that sooner?" The strategic tools are easy to understand. The real challenge consists in embedding these common-sense strategy tools into a strategy.

If, during the reading of this book, you have concentrated on under-standing the strategy concepts and tools, we invite you now to take a large sheet of paper (preferably an A1 sheet or even larger) and to draw with a pencil the strategy process with its nine boxes: performance monitoring, initiating the strategic process, market/company analysis (two boxes), vision, strategy at the three levels (three boxes), and strategy implementation. Now consider your organizational unit – for which you are responsible – as the object of the analysis. For your unit, try to go through each of the nine boxes. How do you measure the performance of your area? Draw a balanced scorecard on the sheet.

What is the state of health of the area? Based on this analysis, which strategic themes must you tackle in the coming months? After that, try in the next box to produce a list of these themes and prioritize them. Then, select one theme and, for this theme, go through the next two boxes. In this analysis phase, describe the market and the company. Afterwards, close your eyes and try to imagine how the ideal world could appear for this selected theme. The subsequent formulation of long-term objectives helps you to revise the vision, in case this has become too unrealistic. After that, consider how the path to the goal must appear to enable the vision to become reality. First of all in general terms, and then in more and more concrete terms, as far as functional strategies and the listing of implementation projects.

The representation of the strategic process on a sheet of paper helps you to reduce the complexity of a situation and to increase the stringency of strategic arguments. Like the top management of 3M, we are convinced that hundreds of PowerPoint slides do not make a strategy. Covering slides with a nicely formatted collection of bullet points does not of itself produce logical consistency. With foil presentations, important relationships can often be lost, and even experienced managers can be misled. What we need is not a scientific analysis of company situations (which, in the last resort, are full of uncertainties), but clear and open discussions concerning the future of the company. Summarize the next PowerPoint presentation in a short piece of prose and avoid analyses that are too detailed. You will immediately get a feeling as to whether the strategy is standing on wobbly legs or is based on a stable foundation. Academics, and sometimes consultants, have in recent years attempted to make an exact science out of the art of strategic company management. The space given to quantitative analyses is out of true proportion in most strategic reports. The English-speaking journals are particularly full of statistical analyses. But the longed-for result of a capability to plan and control in a changing world will not emerge. The striving for apparent certainty all too often replaces business intuition, creativity, and pragmatism.

Therefore, make the attempt to reduce complexity and draw your own strategy map with the nine boxes. You will see that the logic and stringency of the arguments are greatly improved, and that it will become easier for you to preserve the overview – to control the process. If you then find the time once a week in a quiet moment to look at this strategy map and think about the future of the company, there is a good chance that you will increase the quality of your strategic decisions by a very significant factor. Manage your company with the basic principles of the strategy process. Underpin your actions with correct and manageable analysis, develop innovative concepts, and, in particular, put your business heart into the consistent implementation of competitive advantage.

Select Bibliography

Ackermann, F.; Eden, C., *Making Strategy,* Wiltshire, 2000.

Ansoff, I., *Corporate Strategy: An Analytical Approach to Business Policy for Growth and Expansion,* New York, 1965.

Ansoff, I., *Managing Surprise and Discontinuity: Strategic Response to Weak Signals,* European Institute for Advanced Studies in Management (working paper), 1975.

Barney, J., *Gaining and Sustaining Competitive Advantage,* Prentice Hall, New Jersey, 2002.

Bartlett, C.A.; Ghoshal, S., *Going Global: Lessons from Late Movers,* Cambridge/MA, 2000.

Bartlett, C.A.; Ghoshal, S., *Managing Across Borders: The Transnational Solution,* Cambridge/MA, 1989.

Bernstein, Leopold A.; Wild, John J., *Financial Statement Analysis: Theory, Application and Interpretation,* sixth edition, McGraw-Hill, Boston/MA, 1998.

Buzan, T., *The Mind Mapping Book: How to Use Radiant Thinking to Maximise your Brain's Untapped Potential,* Plume, New York, 1993.

Campbell, A., Goold, M., *Corporate-level Strategy: Creating Value in a Multi-Business Company,* New York, 1994.

Charan, R., "Wider eine Kultur der Entschlusslosigkeit", [Against a Culture of Indecisiveness], *Harvard Business Manager,* Vol. 5, S. 34-43, 2001.

Chandler, A., *Strategy and Structure,* Cambridge, 1962.

Courtney, H., "Making the Most out of Uncertainty", *McKinsey Quarterly,* Vol. 4, S. 38-48, 2001.

Courtney, H.; Kirkland, J., "Strategy under Uncertainty", *Harvard Business Review,* November/December, Vol. 75/6, S. 67-81, 1997.

Covey, S., *The 7 Habits of Highly Effective People,* Simon & Schuster, 1989.

Dierickx, I.; Cool, K., "Asset Stock Accumulation and Sustainable Competitive Advantage", *Management Science*, S. 1504-1511, 1989.

Deyhle, A., *Controlling and the Controller: Cost Accounting, Market Planning, Management by Objectives, Role of the Controller,* Gauting Management Service Publications, 1984, rewritten 1992.

Eisenhardt, K.M., "Strategy as Strategic Decision Making", *Sloan Management Review*, Spring, S. 65-72, 1999.

Glaister, Keith W.; Falshaw, I. Richard, "Strategic Planning Still Going Strong?", *Long Range Planning,* Vol. 32, S. 107-116, 1999.

Grant, R., "Resource-based Theory of Competitive Advantage: Implication for Strategy Formulation", *California Management Review,* Vol. 33/3, S. 114-135, 1991.

Grant, R., "Contemporary Strategy Analysis: Concepts, Techniques, Applications", S. 121, Malden/MA, 2002.

Gupta, Anil K.; Govindarajan, Vijav, "Knowledge Flows and the Structure of Control within Multinational Corporations", *Academy of Management Review,* 1991, S. 768-792, 1991.

Hammer, M.; Champy, J., *Re-engineering the Corporation: A Manifesto for Business Revolution,* Harper Business, New York, 1993.

Kaplan, R.S.; Norton, D.P. (1997): *The Balanced Scorecard: Translating Strategy into Action,* Harvard Business School Press, Boston/MA, 1996.

Kotter, J.P., *Leading Chance,* Boston, 1996.

Krystek, U.; Müller-Stewens, C., "Grundzüge einer strategischen Frühaufklärung" [Main Features of Strategic Early Clarification], in: *Strategische Unternehmensplanung – Strategishce Unternehmensführung* [*Strategic Business Planning – Strategic Business Leadership*], Heidelberg, 1990.

Leonard-Barton, D., "Core Capabilities and Core Rigidities: A Paradox in Managing New Product Development", *Strategic Management Journal,* Vol. 13, S. 111-125, 1992.

Leonard-Barton, D., *Wellsprings of Knowledge and Sustaining the Sources of Innovation,* Boston/MA, 1995.

Lewin, K., *Feldtheorie in der Sozialwissenschaft* [Field Theory in the Social Sciences], Bern/Stuttgart, 1963.

Markides, C., *All the Right Moves: A Guide to Crafting Breakthrough Strategy,* Harvard Business School Press, Boston/MA, 2000.

McGee, John; Thomas, Howard, "Strategic Group: Theory, Research and Taxonomy", *Strategic Management Journal,* Vol. 7, S. 141-160, 1986.

Mintzberg, H., *The Decision School: Reconsidering the Basic Promises of Strategic Management,* London, 1990.

Mintzberg, H., *The Rise and Fall of Strategic Planning,* NewYork – London, 1994.

Mintzberg, H., *Strategy Safari: A Guided Tour through the Wilds of Strategic Management,* Free Press, NewYork, 1998.

Müller-Stewens, G.; Lechner, C., *Strategic Management,* Stuttgart, 2001.

von Oetinger, B.; von Ghyczy, T.; Bassford, Ch., *Clausewitzan Strategy: Inspiration and Insight from a Master Strategist,* Wiley, NewYork, 2001.

Porter, M.E., *Competitive Strategy. Techniques for Analyzing Industries and Competitors,* NewYork – London, 1980.

Porter, M.E., "What is Strategy?", *Harvard Business Review,* November-December, S. 61-78, 1996.

Prahalad, C.K.; Bettis, R.A., "The Dominant Logic: A New Linkage between Diversity and Performance", *Strategic Management Journal,* Vol. 7, S. 485-501, 1986.

Pümpin, C., *Strategische Führung in der Unternehmenspraxis* [Strategic Leadership in Business Practice], Bern, 1980.

Quinn, James Brian; Hilmer, Frederick G., "Strategic Outsourcing", *McKinsey Quarterly,* Vol. 1, S. 48-70, 1995.

Quinn, James Brian, *Intelligent Enterprises,* NewYork, 1992.

Rasner, C.; Füser, K.; Faix, W., *Das Existenzgründer-Buch* [The Entrepreneur's Book], Landsberg/Lech, 1997.

Schein, E., "Coming to a New Awareness of Original Culture", *Sloan Management Review,* S. 76-90, 1984.

Shaw, Gordon; Brown, Robert; Bromiley, Philip, "Strategic Stories: How 3M is Rewriting Business Planning", *Harvard Business Review,* May-June, S. 3-8, 1998.

Schoemaker, Paul, J.H., "Scenario Planning: A Tool for Strategic Thinking", *Sloan Management Review,* Vol. 36/2, S. 25-41, 1995.

Simon, H.; von der Gathen, A., *Das große Handbuch der Strategienstrumente. Werkzeuge für eine erfolgreiche Unternehmensführung* [The Handbook of Strategy Instruments: Tools for Successful Business Leadership], Frankfurt – NewYork, 2002.

Venzin, M., "Knowledge Management", *CEMS Business Review,* Vol. 2, S. 205-210, 1998.

Von Krogh, G.; Roos, J., *Organizational Epistemology.* NewYork u. a., 1995.

Index